THE CAJUN VEGAN COOKBOOK

The Cajun Vegan Cookbook

A Modern Guide to Classic Cajun Cooking
& Southern-Inspired Cuisine

KRIMSEY LILLETH

Published by Blue Star Press
PO Box 8835, Bend, OR 97708
contact@bluestarpress.com
www.bluestarpress.com

Photography by Krimsey Lilleth
Cover and Interior Design by Megan Kesting

Disclaimer: This book is for informational and educational purposes. It is not intended
to diagnose, treat, cure, or prevent any disease. Please consult your healthcare provider
before starting or modifying any diet, exercise, or healthcare program.

ISBN: 9781950968473

Printed in China

10 9 8 7 6 5 4 3 2 1

To all of us, who will soon be mushroom food.

Contents

cajun vegan? really? is that even a thing?

That's probably the most common reaction I get whenever I pair those two words together in a sentence. If I'm back home in Louisiana, it usually elicits looks of horror on a few folks' faces, too. Some laugh, some dismiss, some get pissed, and that's all fine by me. Most people come around. There are even a few whose eyes light up when they hear the words "Cajun" and "vegan" together (those are my favorite reactions). No matter what you think at first, this book is for you...because this book is for everyone.

Louisiana's food culture seems to be heavily centered on meat and seafood. However, the key to making great Cajun food isn't either of these things. Sure, meat and seafood are interchangeable ingredients that everyone is familiar with, but they have almost nothing to do with Cajun cuisine's unmistakable flavor.

CAJUN FOOD IS THE SPICES. IT'S THE TECHNIQUE. IT'S THE "THE HOLY TRINITY" (MORE ON THAT LATER).

Not only can "Cajun" and "vegan" go together, but when you marry these two cuisines—one steeped in history and deep flavor, the other ripe with fresh, good-for-you ingredients—you kick open the door to endless new culinary possibilities. Do these Cajun vegan dishes taste exactly like their meat counterparts? Of course not. That would be kind of lame and boring. They are their own things—yummy, interesting, fun things. This is Cajun that won't weigh you down. Frankly put: this is food that doesn't make you feel like crap.

Everything is a choice. Choosing to keep an open mind and try something new can take you to places you didn't even know existed. That's been the story of my life, and it's what brought me to Cajun vegan cooking and where I'm at today.

When I was growing up, I accepted meat as part of my diet. I never questioned it—I just ate what I was given.

I was born in Baton Rouge, Louisiana, and raised in the rich, celebratory culture of the deep South.

I come from a big, blended family and spent much of my childhood roaming outdoors, exploring the area's swampy, magical forests and all the critters that live within them.

I came to really appreciate and respect those living things, and at twenty years old, I learned more about the harsh realities of the animal production industry and decided that I needed to align my diet and lifestyle with my values. Over time, I learned how to eat in a healthy, filling, and delicious way, and I began to share my discoveries with others. It has been a joy watching my friends and family slowly make the transition to more plant-centered ways of living. After all, even an openness to eating just a few fewer meals with meat per week can positively affect your health and the environment in a big way.

I actually worked as a petroleum engineer and project manager for five years before I got into cooking. It was a successful career, and I had a promising future, but over time, I really began struggling with the "why" behind my work. Ethical questions regarding sustainability in the industry plagued me, and I found myself increasingly distracted by dreams of doing something that really mattered to me. Motivated by my desire to help propel the vegan movement forward through positive activism, I made the radical move to abandon my career, pack up my mutt and all my things, and move to California to open my first-ever restaurant: Krimsey's Cajun Kitchen in North Hollywood.

Krimsey's Cajun Kitchen was born in a packed two-bedroom house shared with four roommates and three canine children. Before it was a restaurant, it was a dream housed in a tiny kitchen with only four square feet of counter space. I tinkered for hours and hours, meticulously testing recipes and frequently driving my roommates nuts (but hey...they got to eat the results). It was insane and chaotic, but it was also one of the best years of my life. I'll never forget it.

Eventually I began catering, working farmers' markets and festivals, and writing a cookbook (the early version of what you're now holding in your hands). The more I cooked, the more we all realized that something incredible was brewing. Then on Mardi Gras 2017, I opened my modest little restaurant space on the edge of North Hollywood. With the help of close friends and family, I renovated the space on a shoestring budget and launched the "World's First Cajun Vegan Restaurant!" The concept caught on quickly, and six months later, we expanded into a larger corner space just a few doors down from the original spot.

the restaurant became a hit!

- -

One of the most special things about it was the way it brought people together. I witnessed countless first dates, birthday parties, and family gatherings. We also regularly hosted craft nights (usually hosted by my sister, Jess), live music with "The High Life Cajun Band," Mardi Gras parties, and many other social events. I took great pride in curating an atmosphere that was warm, welcoming, and interesting. The music had to be perfect. The food had to be just right. The "Krewe" (i.e., staff) had to be happy to be at work. And so, I poured myself into it.

I ran and operated Krimsey's Cajun Kitchen for about three years, and when COVID-19 hit in the spring of 2020, I had a big decision to make. I just knew that it was going to last a while. As I tried to peer into the future, I saw months (maybe years?) of trouble, or at best, a version of the restaurant without all the community that had sprung up around it. Running a restaurant is already a tough job, and without the perks of community interaction, craft nights, live music, and Mardi Gras parties, I had a hard time seeing the point. I didn't want to be a takeout business, so I closed up shop and began looking for my next project. I'd taken many risks before, so I wasn't too concerned about taking on one more. I knew it would be okay, and I'd eventually find something incredible to work on. Not too long after the painful decision to close our doors, a former customer who works for a publishing company reached out about publishing my Cajun vegan cookbook. I was stoked, and here we are.

Food is life. It's something we all need to survive, and every time we take a bite, we make choices. Do we love ourselves? Do we respect ourselves? Do we respect other creatures? For me, modernizing Cajun cuisine through my vegan cooking is a way to honor the culture back home while updating it so that it can be preserved and enjoyed for generations to come, particularly as more people adopt a plant-based diet and become aware of how harmful animal products can be to our health, our environment, and the animals themselves.

Health has never been much of a consideration when cooking "Louisiana style," but all my Cajun vegan recipes are 100 percent cholesterol-free, low in saturated fat, and generally lower in calories than their omnivorous alternatives. Sure, I use vegan butter (it's delicious). But overall, these recipes are massively better for our health than old-style Cajun cooking. I want us all to live long, happy, and healthy lives, and I think better food choices are what's going to get us there.

When I adopted a vegan diet in 2007, I was clueless about how to cook good food without using meat, dairy, or eggs. Over the years, though, I have mastered the art. Now it's my pleasure to pass my knowledge and passion for this lifestyle on to you.

For whatever reason, this book has ended up in your hands: Whether you grabbed it with excitement when you read the words "Cajun" and "vegan" on the cover; whether you thought, "that can't be done," or "can that be any good?"; or whether someone thrust this book in your hands and said, "read this!"—whoever you are and however you got here, thank you. You've made the choice to read this far, and I hope you choose to continue on with me. I am grateful for your interest, and if you're skeptical, I'm ready for the challenge and excited to embark on this journey of showing you that, yes, "Cajun vegan" food is a thing—

and it's freakin' delicious.

Stocking Your Kitchen

Certain ingredients are absolutely essential to authentic-tasting Cajun cooking. Most traditional recipes build on flavor profiles that start with these items and just wouldn't be the same without them.

Below are some that you'll repeatedly see throughout this cookbook.

THE HOLY TRINITY—CELERY, ONION, AND GREEN BELL PEPPERS

This forms the flavor base for many Cajun and Creole dishes, and you'll see this veggie combo in many of the recipes in this book. These days, garlic is also usually considered a part of the Trinity, but it's called a "Trinity," not a "Quaternity," so sorry, garlic—you're the fourth wheel for now.

CAJUN SEASONING—A SPECIAL BLEND OF SPICES

Essential to most Cajun recipes; you can make it yourself (page 193) or get a generic version from most grocery stores. Just watch out for cheap impostors—many brands like to skimp on expensive ingredients (like white pepper) and sub in salt, which leads to a less dynamic flavor profile. If you use store-bought Cajun seasoning, your recipes won't taste exactly like the ones in this book, but they'll be close. Just watch the salt—using store-bought Cajun seasoning may mean you don't need to add any extra salt as instructed in the recipes.

ROUX—ROASTED FLOUR/OIL COMBO

Made from a simple roasted flour/oil combo, this base is used to bring flavor depth and that "Cajun uniqueness" to dishes like gumbo, étouffée, and many other traditional recipes. No two roux are created equal, though. From light roux to dark roux, they all bring something special to the table. The key to making roux is to take it slow. Rice flour can be used to make it gluten-free and will be almost indistinguishable from the original wheat-based version. You can also roast a roux in the oven, but I don't recommend it for beginners—it's easy to burn, and it can make a mess. It also changes the flavor profile a bit (it's noticeable). So all of my recipes here use the stovetop method.

Suggested PANTRY ITEMS

Cajun vegan cooking tends to follow certain flavor themes, so below are some other items you'll want to have stocked in your kitchen. I've also included items that are just generally good to have on hand for all recipes, as well as an introduction to any "weird" ingredients you may not recognize if you're new to vegan cooking.

DAIRY-ISH ITEMS

Non-Dairy Milk (Unsweetened)
Vegan Butter
Vegan Mayo
Vegan Cheese

MEAT-ISH ITEMS

Vegan Beef Crumbles
Vegan Sausage
Tofu
Hearts of Palm

OTHER

Parboiled Rice
Hot Sauce
Vegan Worcestershire Sauce
Liquid Smoke
Bragg Liquid Aminos
Oils
Apple Cider Vinegar
Sweeteners
Cornmeal
Cajun Seasoning & Dried Spices
Nutritional Yeast
Bouillon Cubes
Tapioca Starch
Baking Ingredients

NON-DAIRY MILK (UNSWEETENED) Different non-dairy milks contribute different flavors, textures, and cooking properties to a recipe. For example, oat milk tends to be thicker and emulsifies better, and brings a relatively strong flavor with it (in my opinion). I tend to prefer rice milk because it's got a pretty neutral flavor, is liquidy but not incredibly watery, and is allergen-friendly, in case you're cooking for anyone with nut allergies. It can also be stored unopened in the pantry. If you don't want to (or can't) use rice milk, I recommend subbing in almond milk or coconut milk—the kind that comes in a carton meant for drinking, not canned coconut milk. No matter your preference, I always recommend opting for unsweetened non-dairy milk because it's the best way to level the sweetness playing field and then build from there according to the original recipe.

VEGAN BUTTER Similar to margarine, vegan butter can be found in most chain grocery stores these days. If you can't get vegan butter, you can generally sub in vegetable oil, olive oil, or vegetable shortening in my recipes.

VEGAN MAYO Traditional mayo contains egg. Thankfully, there are now many brands of vegan mayo available, so take your pick.

VEGAN CHEESE There are so many great vegan cheeses on the market these days, and I bet you'll be pleasantly surprised by their flavor. No, they're not exactly like real cheese, and no, they don't always melt the same, but can I get an "amen!" for progress? The stuff available these days is miles ahead of where we were just a few years ago. It seems like a new vegan cheese hits the market every month, and I'm not complaining.

VEGAN BEEF CRUMBLES There are several brands making vegan beef crumbles (like taco meat) these days. You can find them in the frozen and meat sections of the store in the sections labeled "plant-based." Just make sure you're picking a vegan one—some brands still add eggs and milk for some reason, but I believe they'll come around eventually.

VEGAN SAUSAGE With the advancements in plant-based meats, there are some vegan sausages on the market now that are so good you won't even be able to tell they aren't the real thing. Look for brands like Field Roast Sausages or Beyond Sausages stocked in the meat aisle of most supermarkets. As with vegan beef crumbles, just make sure to look for the section of the store labeled "plant-based."

TOFU If you've never tried tofu before, or have tasted it but been kinda iffy about the flavor or texture, remember: it's all about how you cook it. I've got some great recipes and tips throughout this book that I hope will turn you into a fan. There are a few different options available, but I recommend purchasing extra-firm tofu blocks, unless a recipe calls for silken tofu. The latter is usually found in the Asian section of stores (not the plant-based section) and has a different flavor and texture.

HEARTS OF PALM Harvested from palm trees in South and Central America, heart of palm is a white flesh that resembles artichoke and often comes canned. For all of the recipes in this book, I've used canned hearts of palm because I like the brined taste and texture. You could use fresh palm, but I don't recommend it. Note that these palm trees are different from the trees used to harvest controversial palm oil. Heart of palm generally comes from coconut, juçara, açaí, palmetto, or peach palm trees. Palm oil, on the other hand, is harvested from the African oil palm tree—a totally different species in a totally different place.

PARBOILED RICE Parboiling is the secret to fluffy, delicious rice that is still good for you. It tastes a lot like white rice, but has nearly all (about 80 percent) of the nutrients found in brown rice. This has to do with the way they process it: Parboiled rice is soaked, steamed, and dried all before removing the husk. During steaming, the nutrients are driven from the bran to the endosperm so that when the husk is removed, the nutrients remain with the rice! Parboiled rice is one of my top kitchen secrets that usually changes everyone's rice-cooking experiences for the better. I bet after trying parboiled rice, you'll never want to cook white or brown rice again.

HOT SAUCE What would a good Cajun dish be without a little extra kick? My favorite hot sauce brands are Tabasco, Crystal, and my family's secret-recipe hot sauce (sorry, not giving that away in this book!). Each sauce has its own flavor profile and may work better with some dishes than others, but they can all typically be used interchangeably. Just try to avoid sauces with added sugar! If I recommend a specific sauce for a certain dish, I'll let you know in the ingredients list.

VEGAN WORCESTERSHIRE SAUCE Most Worcestershire contains fish and/or anchovies, but many brands are beginning to omit it. Watch out for those sneaky fishy ingredients when you're picking up this sauce at the store.

LIQUID SMOKE Found in the barbecue sauce section of most grocery stores, liquid smoke gives recipes a smoky flavor similar to what you'd get if you were actually cooking with wood. Usually, recipes only call for a tiny amount, so it's tempting to skip it, but trust me: that little bit of flavor makes all the difference.

BRAGG LIQUID AMINOS A tasty unprocessed alternative to soy and tamari sauce. If you can't find Bragg in your local store, then soy or tamari will work just fine.

OILS I usually recommend canola oil for frying, vegetable oil for baking, and olive oil for sautéing. You can mostly use all of these interchangeably depending on your preferences, except when it comes to frying. If you want to use a different oil for frying, pick one with a high enough smoke point to hold up to frying heats—and pick one that gives you a little wiggle room in case you accidentally overheat it. Avocado oil and peanut oil are good alternatives to canola.

APPLE CIDER VINEGAR I mostly add apple cider vinegar to recipes for acidity, but it also brings a woody, sour flavor to dishes that you won't get with plain ol' vinegar.

SWEETENERS Maple syrup and molasses are a few other versatile essentials you'll see throughout this book in everything from biscuits to gumbo.

CORNMEAL I recommend a version of cornmeal that is finely ground for making softer baked goods, but a coarse version has its merits, too. Your final product will just feel a little more "rustic" and crumbly.

CAJUN SEASONING Like I said earlier, no Cajun kitchen is complete without this essential spice. You can buy it at the store, but I highly recommend making your own using my recipe on page 193.

DRIED SPICES Cayenne pepper, garlic powder, onion powder, freshly cracked black pepper, and salt are all frequently called for in this cookbook and good to have ready to go.

NUTRITIONAL YEAST A unique, savory ingredient that adds a nutty or cheesy flavor to recipes, nutritional yeast can usually be found in the vitamin aisles of health stores like Whole Foods, or sometimes with the spices (this is more common lately). Nutritional yeast can also be used as a B12 supplement, but if you're looking for that extra boost, make sure you pick a nutritional yeast brand that is fortified with the vitamin—not all have it.

BOUILLON CUBES Not-Chick'n brand bouillon cubes add crazy good flavor to dishes in place of animal-based broths! If you can't find them, just stick with liquid veggie stock. I've even been seeing liquid "no-chicken broth" popping up in stores lately, so that would work well too.

TAPIOCA STARCH Also known as tapioca flour, it's used as a binding agent and works well to thicken sauces and soups.

BAKING INGREDIENTS All-purpose flour, baking powder, cane sugar, cornstarch, and brown sugar are all versatile and essential for a lot of the desserts and fried items in this cookbook.

Gluten-free?

Many of the recipes in this cookbook are naturally gluten-free, and we've included GF symbols on those recipes so you can easily find them. As time goes on, I am beginning to see gluten-free flour blends pop up in stores that you can sub in one-to-one for wheat flour. However, baking with gluten-free flour is usually going to produce a significantly different experience than using wheat-based flour. Unless you are a seasoned gluten-free baker or are using a blend specifically designated as a one-to-one flour substitute, I caution you against attempting too many substitutions in your baked goodies.

For savory dishes involving roux, you can easily make them gluten-free by simply using white rice flour as a roux base instead of wheat flour. It's not exactly the same, but it's pretty damn close. The main difference I notice when making a gluten-free roux is that it tends to sort of "puff up" a little more than standard roux as it's stored. If you're making it the day of, the difference is hardly noticeable, even to an experienced cook!

LOOK FOR THE GF LOGO ON THE RECIPE PAGES

 GLUTEN-FREE

 RECIPE CAN BE MODIFIED

Suggested Tools

Below are some kitchen tools that I've discovered over the years and now cannot cook without.

CAST-IRON SKILLET A standard tool in any Cajun or Southern kitchen, a cast-iron skillet is a heavy-duty pan that has a very high heat capacity. There's an art to using one, and I've got a guide on page 18 to get you started. If you don't have one and aren't ready to make the purchase, don't worry. You can use a regular skillet for any recipe that calls for cast iron. It won't be exactly the same, but it will be close and you'll be fine.

FOOD SCOOPER I have a 0.86-ounce food service scooper (also known as a #40 scoop) with a release handle that works great for sticky dessert doughs and recipes like hushpuppies. I highly recommend spending a few bucks on this tool—it's very useful!

FRYING THERMOMETER This is a necessity for making fried items. Some cooks recommend the "wooden spoon" test (dipping a wooden spoon in to see if it makes bubbles to determine if the oil is hot enough), but it's not exact. Getting a frying thermometer will make your frying experience so much more predictable and enjoyable. Even if you have a mini electric fryer, I still recommend using a frying thermometer to double-check temperatures. I find that those mini home fryers don't actually reach the temperatures they're supposed to. For more on frying, see page 21.

GARLIC PRESS When a recipe calls for "minced garlic," pressed garlic works too. What I love about a garlic press is that you don't have to peel the clove! You can just shove it in and go. You'll get a little more "garlic meat" out if you peel first, but for me, it's worth it to skip the peeling and just shove an extra in to make up for it. Peeling garlic is the worst.

OVEN THERMOMETER If you have an older oven, it may not be working at the exact temperature you think it is. A small investment in an oven thermometer can help ensure that you don't waste your valuable time over- or undercooking dishes because your oven isn't performing how it should be. Trust me...this sucks.

PASTRY WHEEL AND ROLLING PIN These make pastry work so much easier. If you're planning to make pies, breakfast pastries, or beignets, I'd highly recommend getting both of these items. The rolling pin you're probably familiar with, but the pastry wheel is for cutting clean dough lines, in case you're wondering—much easier than a knife.

RICE COOKER Sure, you can always cook your rice in a pot over the stove, but investing in a rice cooker was one of the best things I ever did for my sanity in the kitchen. It makes consistently perfect rice without having to watch or stir it.

ROUX SPOON This is just any type of flat-bottomed spoon. I prefer wood, but metal works too so long as you're not working with a nonstick pan—it will definitely scratch your pan. A flat-bottomed spoon is useful because it allows you to really scrape the bottom of a pot to avoid things sticking, which is especially important for roux!

BLENDER AND FOOD PROCESSOR These are essential for sauces, drinks, and the occasional dessert.

BAKING PAN, MUFFIN PAN, LOAF DISH, AND PIE DISH Nothing is more annoying than getting in the mood for baking and realizing you don't have the right tools. Keep these on hand and you'll cover your bases.

COOKIE CUTTERS AND BISCUIT CUTTERS I find myself using these all the time. Some like to use a pastry wheel or the rim of a drinking glass to cut dough, but having the right cutting tools creates a final product that fluffs up better with more precise edges.

STAR ICING TIP You can always put icing in a plastic bag and cut off the corner to distribute, but a star icing tip will help you create a more professional design.

MINI SPATULA Sure, you'll use a regular-sized spatula for most things in the kitchen, but having a mini one is great for when you're making smaller sweet treats like the Salted Pecan Pralines on page 233.

TOOTHPICKS AND SHISH KABOB STICKS These are useful for holding food in place, like the Mini Festival Corn Dogs on page 105 or the to-die-for Fresh Tomato Bloody Mary on page 263.

Cast-Iron Cooking

Most of the recipes in this book are written for people using non-cast-iron pans, but cast-iron cooking is classically Southern and practically any recipe in this book can be cooked with one. You'll just need to preheat your pan well and possibly adjust your heat level and cooking time to account for the material differences (more about that later in this section).

I love cooking breads and desserts with cast iron. The material holds heat very well and leads to an even cooking temperature all around, so long as it's preheated properly. I also love the nostalgic feeling of cooking with cast iron—it makes me feel like I'm in my great-great-grandmother's kitchen. If well taken care of, cast-iron cookware can also last for decades. However, there are a few things to be aware of when cooking with cast iron.

If you're trying to completely avoid all animal products in your kitchen, check that the manufacturer used a vegetable-based oil to season the pan. Many cast-iron skillets come "pre-seasoned," which means that the manufacturer applied some sort of oil or fat over the surface of the cast iron and heated it to a high temperature. This caused the oil to "polymerize," or break down into a plastic-like material that bonded to the surface of the cast iron. In the past, many suppliers used lard to season pans, but that is becoming less common these days as many switch to vegan-friendly alternatives. But if you're worried about it, just reach out to the manufacturer and check!

If your new pan did not come pre-seasoned, you'll need to do it yourself! It's pretty simple. I've tried a lot of different methods.

Here's What Works Best For Me ☛

ONE—SCRUB

Scrub your new cast-iron pan with warm, soapy water and then towel it off. Set aside to dry for a few hours. If you're in a hurry, heat it on the stove on medium-low heat for about 10 minutes to evaporate any leftover moisture. Allow the pan to cool completely before proceeding.

TWO—PREHEAT OVEN TO 400°

THREE—OIL

Once the pan is thoroughly dry, use a gloved hand or lint-free towel to spread oil all over the pan—inside, outside, and on the handle. I use canola oil, but you can also use vegetable oil or vegetable shortening. It shouldn't be dripping oil, but it should be covered lightly. In this case, less is more. There should be no chunks or streaks; the goal is to have a smooth, thin layer. Wait 5 minutes and then give it another rub with oil, covering any dry-looking spots.

FOUR—PLACE IN OVEN

Place your oiled pan into the oven (inverted with the interior cooking surface downward) with a drip pan or sheet of foil beneath it to catch any oil drippings. But if you went light on the oil, you shouldn't have any drippings—that's the goal!

FIVE—BAKE

Bake the pan for 1 hour, then turn off the oven and allow the pan to cool inside the oven slowly. When it's cooled, it's ready to use. Some people like to run it through another round of baking, but personally I find that one round is usually sufficient. However, if you notice uncovered spots, give it another round.

TIP The oven might smoke a bit. I recommend opening all your doors and windows and getting some fans going to keep the air in your house fresh.

CLEANING YOUR CAST-IRON Cast iron is a very durable material, but there are some things to know about cleaning this type of pan.

As soon as you're done cooking, use warm water and a bit of salt or baking soda with a nylon dish brush or scrubby sponge (not steel wool) to clean the pan, neutralize flavors/odors, and kill bacteria. If your pan got a little extra dirty while cooking, or the baking soda isn't cleaning well enough, use a little dish soap and scrub gently (it's okay, it won't hurt your pan). Just avoid putting it in the dishwasher or using harsh cleaners. You'll notice that the more you cook with it, the more you'll build up a nonstick surface, and it will become even easier to clean.

Never soak your cast-iron pan in water. It is prone to rusting, so remember to dry thoroughly after washing. If you ever notice bits of rust on your cast iron, don't worry—it happens. Use some steel wool to scrape off the rust, then go through the seasoning process again to recoat your pan in polymerized oil.

COOKING WITH YOUR CAST-IRON Your cast-iron pan can take basically whatever you throw at it! You can use a metal spatula or pretty much any other type of utensil without fear of it damaging your pan. Just be careful with acidic food (like tomatoes) and sugary desserts. Avoid cooking them for long times in the pan, at least until you've built up a really solid layer of seasoning. Short cook times work, but a long simmer could cause iron to leach into your food and break down your seasoning layer. You won't die (probably), but your food will taste like metal.

Although cast iron holds heat well, it is terrible at distributing that heat quickly. That is why it is important to preheat the cast iron if you're using it on a burner to avoid hot spots. Just set it over medium-low heat for 10 minutes and you'll be ready to cook.

Your cast-iron cookware will likely get much hotter than other cookware over the exact same heat (because it holds heat so

well), so go light on the heat if you're not used to cooking with it. Gradually increase the heat once you see that nothing is burning! Generally, low to medium heat is sufficient for cooking with cast iron.

Over time, you may notice dull spots or feel that the pan is not as dark as it once was overall. It's probably just due for another seasoning session. Every time you cook with cast iron, you're adding new polymerized oils to the skillet, which adds more layers of seasoning over time. Eventually, your cast iron will become a shiny black cooking treasure.

If you choose to cook with cast iron, I hope you have as much fun with it as I do! It also makes for beautiful food photos, if you're into that.

Me cooking with my self-seasoned, 15-gallon cast-iron jambalaya pot.

Frying for Beginners

Sure, we can all probably agree that eating fried foods every day isn't a good idea. But they're a fun treat.

If you're new to frying, the most important thing to know is that it's not that hard. The whole process can actually be pretty pain-free. If you want the easiest option, invest in a good mini electric fryer. Definitely spend the money on a high-quality version, though, because these countertop fryers sometimes overpromise and underdeliver. I recommend that you still double-check the oil temperature with a frying thermometer for this reason, just to be safe.

IF YOU'D RATHER DO THINGS THE OLD-FASHIONED WAY WITH A POT AND SOME OIL OVER THE STOVE, THAT WORKS TOO.

1. Choose a pot that's tall and skinny. This will help keep oil from spraying all over your kitchen, and the "skinny" part will reduce the amount of oil you need to create the right oil level in your pot. Trust me, always go taller for frying!

2. If you're a first-time fryer, line the areas around your burner with aluminum foil. It's hard not to make a mess your first time, and this will make the process feel less stressful so you can focus on your food.

3. Put your burner on medium heat and let the oil heat up fully. I usually turn on the burner and let it heat for at least 20 minutes. For me, the perfect frying temperature (375°F) is at about a 6 out of 10 on my burner, but yours may be a bit different. There are a lot of factors, from the size and shape of your pot to the oil volume to your burner strength, that can all affect the perfect burner setting for you. Check the temperature with a frying thermometer, and slowly adjust your burner heat as needed.

4. If you do not have a frying thermometer, you can use the "wooden spoon" method: Dip a wooden spoon in the fryer oil for two seconds. If you notice tiny bubbles forming and swimming around the spoon, it's the right temperature for frying (about 375°F). If large, aggressive bubbles begin forming, your oil is probably too hot. Lower the burner heat slightly and continue testing the temperature with your wooden spoon. Since this is not an exact way to

heat your oil to a certain temperature, you'll have to watch your goodies a little closer and adjust the cooking time as needed to achieve golden-brown results.

5. If frying with a wet batter, use two pairs of tongs: one for dropping food in the oil, and another pair for pulling food out of the oil. This will keep you from building up cooked batter on the tips of your tongs (which is annoying).

6. Between frying rounds, let the oil heat back up for about 60 seconds before adding new items, because the temperature will naturally drop a bit as the food absorbs the heat.

7. Skim any debris off the top of the oil frequently. Those little bits of batter can burn and make your oil (and foods you're frying in it) taste bitter and charred.

8. Please be careful! Frying oil is hot (shocker) and can pop, sizzle, and fry your skin off. As tempting as it is, don't use your hands to drop things into the oil. Or do (it's your prerogative), but just know I warned you!

9. Frying oil can be used many times, so long as you skim the oil regularly to keep it in good shape. When it's time to toss out, I recommend taking it down to a local waste center that accepts grease for recycling. Or you can let it cool completely, transfer it to a non-breakable container, and put it in the trash. Don't pour it down the sink—it's bad for your pipes and for the environment.

Soaking BEANS

Beans are common in Southern cooking (red beans, anyone?), and even more so in my vegan Southern cooking. They're hearty flavor-carriers that are packed with nutrients. Sometimes, canned beans work just fine for me. But generally, I prefer the taste and texture of home-cooked beans. I can also control the salt content when cooking dry beans, which I appreciate. It just depends on what you prefer—convenience is an important factor for many, and the taste difference is subtle. So choose what works for you.

If you do decide to cook your own beans, that raises the age-old question...soak the beans, or not? It seems like everyone has a different opinion. Personally, I like to soak my beans because it's not that hard, and it shortens the cooking time slightly. The flavor and texture effects are minor, but I notice them. Also, beans can really dry out in the pantry sometimes, so soaking them will help bring all beans to the same hydration level before cooking so that the recipe works consistently, no matter how old and dry the beans may be.

On a health note, some believe that soaking beans is healthier because it releases the phytic acid found in them. In your digestive system, phytic acid binds to minerals like zinc, iron, magnesium, calcium, chromium, and manganese and keeps you from fully absorbing them. However, soaking also releases the minerals themselves from the beans, so the evidence that soaking is healthier overall is unclear—it may be a net-zero gain. But maybe by the time this book comes out, we'll know more. I encourage you to do your own research and come to your own conclusion.

Some people argue that soaking doesn't do anything in any capacity (taste, texture, or healthwise), and you're wasting your time. And soaking's effectiveness seems to vary from one bean to the another. So long story short: Skip soaking if it's not your jam. You'll just need to cook them a bit longer than my recipes call for, and you might need a little extra water, too.

If You Do Choose To Soak Your Beans,
HERE'S HOW YOU DO IT

1. Rinse your dry beans in a colander and pick out any foreign objects (rocks, sticks, etc.). It's rare, but debris does make it in sometimes!

2. Transfer your rinsed beans to a large pot and cover with water. The water should reach at least 3 inches above the beans, because they will expand significantly.

3. Cover your pot and allow the beans to soak at room temperature for at least 6–12 hours

4. Drain off the excess water and your beans are ready to use in your recipe!

If you completely forgot to soak, don't fret. You'll just need to add 10–25 minutes to your total recipe cooking time to make up for the lack of pre-soak. You'll also probably need to add a little extra water during the cooking process. But overall, the flavor and texture of the dish will be mostly the same, and still delicious!

You may have heard of something called "quick soaking," but I don't recommend it. The procedure is to basically quick-boil the beans and then let them sit for an hour before using, but I don't get the point. You might as well just add a little extra cooking time to your dish and skip the soaking altogether.

Let's **GET STARTED**

Pumpkin Oat Breakfast Bread
with Maple Hunny Butter

breakfast &
BREADS

savory corn, bacon, & cheese **PANCAKES**

Yes, savory pancakes are a thing! To me, these pancakes almost feel like eating an omelet, but *better* because there's maple syrup and butter involved.

STUFF YOU NEED

1 cup all-purpose flour

½ cup cornmeal

¼ cup tapioca starch

1 tablespoon cane sugar

1 tablespoon baking powder

½ teaspoon salt

¼ teaspoon Krimsey's Cajun Seasoning (page 193)

1 tablespoon vegan butter, melted, plus extra for greasing the pan

1 cup plus 2 tablespoon unsweetened non-dairy milk (rice milk recommended)

½ cup corn kernels

½ cup shredded vegan cheddar cheese

¼ cup Smoky Maple Bacon Bits (page 196)

Recommended toppings: sliced green onions, freshly cracked black pepper, vegan butter, and maple syrup

WHAT TO DO

1. Whisk together the flour, cornmeal, tapioca starch, sugar, baking powder, salt, and Cajun seasoning in a medium bowl.

2. Add vegan butter and non-dairy milk. Mix well until no clumps remain. Gently fold in corn, vegan cheese, and Smoky Maple Bacon Bits. Don't overmix, just stir until well-combined and then let it rest for 5–10 minutes (but no more!) while your pan heats up.

3. Heat an electric griddle (recommended) to 365°F or heat a frying pan over medium-low heat. I know 365°F for the griddle sounds oddly specific, but trust me. I've made a lot of pancakes and this is the temperature that gives me consistently fluffy pancakes with yummy brown and slightly crunch outsides.

4. Once heated, throw down ½ teaspoon of vegan butter per pancake (recommended), or coat the pan lightly with nonstick spray.

5. Scoop ¼ cup of batter per pancake onto the pan. Cook until edges look firm and little bubbles form in the middle of the pancake, 2–2½ minutes. Use a spatula to peek underneath—the bottom of each pancake should be light golden brown with darker edges and lines throughout before you flip.

6. Flip and cook for another 1½–2 minutes on the other side.

7. Once pancakes are cooked throughout, remove from the heat and taste test. Adjust the heat settings if needed and repeat the process with the rest of your batter.

7. Add preferred toppings and enjoy this savory breakfast treat.

southern diner **PANCAKES**

For most of us, pancakes remind us of childhood, no matter where we came from. Growing up in the South, I always assumed pancakes must be a Southern thing (I thought we were really special), but it turns out everyone loves them. So here's a vegan version of the diner-style pancakes that I used to drool over at our post-church brunch spot. This is a solid base recipe, so try mixing in your favorite add-ins to create your own fun twist on this recipe. P.S. I nearly finished this entire stack of pancakes after the photo shoot.

STUFF YOU NEED

1¼ cups all-purpose flour

¼ cup tapioca starch

2 tablespoons cane sugar

1 tablespoon baking powder

½ teaspoon salt

1¼ cups unsweetened non-dairy milk
    (rice milk recommended)

2 tablespoons vegan butter, melted,
    plus extra for greasing the pan

1 teaspoon vanilla extract

Optional add-ins: vegan chocolate chips, mashed banana, chopped walnuts, finely diced apples

Toppings: maple syrup, vegan butter, and fresh-cut fruit

WHAT TO DO

1. Whisk together the flour, tapioca starch, sugar, baking powder, and salt in a medium bowl.

2. Add non-dairy milk, vegan butter, vanilla extract, and any optional add-ins. Use a spatula to mix until no clumps remain, but don't go crazy—just mix until it's smooth and then leave it alone. Once combined, let it rest while your griddle or pan heats up (5–10 minutes, max).

3. Heat an electric griddle (recommended) to 365°F, or heat a frying pan over medium-low heat. I know 365°F for the griddle sounds oddly specific, but trust me. I've made a lot of pancakes and this is the temperature that gives me consistently fluffy pancakes with yummy brown and slightly crunchy outsides.

4. Once your surface is heated, throw down ½ teaspoon of vegan butter per pancake (recommended) or coat the pan lightly with nonstick spray.

5. Scoop ¼ cup of batter per pancake onto the pan. Cook until edges look firm and little bubbles form in the middle of the pancake, 2–2½ minutes. Use a spatula to peek underneath—the bottom of each pancake should be light golden brown with darker edges and lines throughout before you flip.

6. Flip and cook for another 1½–2 minutes on the other side.

7. Once pancakes are cooked throughout, remove from the heat and taste test. Adjust the heat settings if needed, and repeat the process with the rest of your batter.

8. Top with vegan butter while pancakes are still warm and serve with maple syrup and fresh fruit!

molasses & roasted pecan PANCAKES

The pre-roasted and salted pecans give these slightly sweet pancakes a soft crunch and roasted flavor. You can sub in raw pecans, but I highly recommend taking a few extra minutes to roast the pecans beforehand; your future self will be glad you did.

STUFF YOU NEED

1¼ cups all-purpose flour

¼ cup tapioca starch

2 tablespoons packed light brown sugar

1 tablespoon baking powder

1 teaspoon ground cinnamon

½ teaspoon salt

1¼ cups unsweetened non-dairy milk (rice milk recommended)

2 tablespoons vegan butter, melted, plus extra for greasing the pan

1 tablespoon unsulphured molasses

1 teaspoon vanilla extract

½ cup plus 2 tablespoons Roasted & Salted Pecans (page 197), crumbled

Recommended toppings: maple syrup, vegan butter, Roasted & Salted Pecans, and powdered sugar

WHAT TO DO

1. Whisk together the flour, tapioca starch, brown sugar, baking powder, cinnamon, and salt in a medium mixing bowl.

2. Add non-dairy milk, vegan butter, molasses, and vanilla extract. Mix well until no clumps remain—no need to beat it to death. Fold in ½ cup of the pecan crumbles, and set the rest aside for later. Stir until pecan crumbles are evenly dispersed in the batter, then let it rest for 5–10 minutes (but no more than that) while you heat up your griddle or pan.

3. Heat an electric griddle (recommended) to 365°F, or heat a frying pan over medium-low heat.

4. Once heated, throw down ½ teaspoon of vegan butter per pancake (recommended), or coat the pan lightly with nonstick spray. Put ½ teaspoon crumbled pecans in the very center of where you plan to pour each pancake.

5. Pour ¼ cup batter over the pecan pile. This will make the tops of your pancakes look extra pretty while also browning some of the pecans for flavor. Just watch out for large pieces here—pieces that are too big could prevent the batter behind them from fully cooking through.

6. Cook until edges look firm and little bubbles form in the middle of the pancakes, 2–2½ minutes. Use a spatula to peek underneath—the bottom of each pancake should be light golden brown with darker edges and lines throughout before you flip.

7. Flip and cook for another 1½–2 minutes on the other side.

8. Once cooked throughout, remove pancakes from the heat and taste test. Adjust the heat settings if needed, and repeat the process with the rest of your batter and pecan crumbles. You may not use all 2 tablespoons of pecan crumbles; that's okay.

9. Finish with preferred toppings and serve immediately.

Having lived in "country" places for most of my youth, bonfires were a consistent presence in many of my favorite memories. When I found out marshmallows weren't vegan, I was devastated. If you already knew this, you understand my pain; if you didn't know, Google "how gelatin is made" (cue gagging). Thankfully, vegan marshmallows exist now; they hit the market shortly after my transition into veganism, and I began using them as often as possible—even in breakfast.

STUFF YOU NEED

Wet Batter Dip

- ¾ cup unsweetened non-dairy milk (rice milk recommended)
- ¼ cup plus 2 tablespoons vegan butter, melted
- 1½ tablespoons cornstarch
- 1 teaspoon vanilla extract
- ½ teaspoon salt

Filling

- ¼ cup vegan butter, melted
- ¼ cup brown sugar
- 1 teaspoon ground cinnamon
- 1 cup vegan mini marshmallows
- ¼ cup vegan mini chocolate chips*

Coating

- 4 teaspoons cane sugar
- 2 teaspoons light brown sugar brown sugar
- ½ teaspoon ground cinnamon
- 10–12 large slices soft white bread**

For serving: Maple syrup

Notes: *Check the ingredients in the chocolate chips to make sure they're dairy-free! **Also, I specify large, soft bread slices because in order to roll up the French toast without losing your mind, you want to have a big, soft canvas.

WHAT TO DO

1. In a small, shallow bowl, whisk together all wet batter dip ingredients.

2. In another small bowl, mix together all filling ingredients except mini marshmallows and mini chocolate chips.

3. In a wide, shallow bowl or plate, mix both sugars and cinnamon together for your coating. Set aside.

4. Cut the crusts off bread slices to make rectangles, but try to conserve as much bread canvas as possible. Divide filling evenly among bread slices and spread over the top of each slice.

5. Heat an electric griddle to 400°F, or heat a nonstick skillet over medium-high heat.

6. Line up some mini marshmallows along the long edge of each slice of bread—that will be the middle of your roll. Sprinkle ½ teaspoon of chocolate chips in a line next to the marshmallows, then roll up bread starting at the marshmallow side. If it's difficult to roll, your bread slice might be a bit small. Just flip the orientation on the next one, lining up the marshmallows and rolling starting on the short edge of the bread. This will give you more runway for rolling up the French toast.

7. Dip each roll in wet batter and shake off excess liquid. Transfer roll to your ungreased hot pan or griddle with the seam side down. Cook for about 1 minute, then rotate and cook on the other 3 sides for about 1 minute each as well, or until dark brown edges show up.

8. When all sides are done, remove French toast from the heat and roll in the cinnamon-sugar coating. Set aside and continue with the rest of your roll-ups.

9. Serve warm with maple syrup.

classic french TOAST

This dish is so versatile when it comes to how it can be served. My favorite version at my restaurant was to top it with sautéed sausage, Smoky Maple Bacon Bits, Candied Pecan Pieces, powdered sugar, Maple Hunny Butter, and maple syrup. Classic.

STUFF YOU NEED

1 cup unsweetened non-dairy milk (rice milk recommended)

¼ cup vegan butter, melted, plus extra for greasing the pan

¾ cup all-purpose flour

⅓ cup cane sugar

1 tablespoon ground cinnamon

1½ teaspoons vanilla extract

½ teaspoon salt

½ teaspoon ground nutmeg

8–12 slices bread, any shape or size*

Recommended toppings: Candied Pecan Pieces (page 199), Smoky Maple Bacon Bits (page 196), Maple Hunny Butter (page 188), powdered sugar, maple syrup, vegan cream cheese, vegan sausage slices, sliced strawberries, bananas, blueberries, or apples

Note: *If your bread slices are on the bigger and thicker side, your batter may run short and you'll wind up with fewer cooked slices, of course.

WHAT TO DO

1. In a medium bowl, whisk together non-dairy milk and melted vegan butter. Add all remaining batter ingredients (but don't put the bread in yet).

2. Heat an electric griddle to 400°F, or heat a large skillet over medium-high heat.

3. Melt ½ teaspoon of butter in the pan, then dip a piece of bread into the batter, turning to coat. Shake off excess liquid and transfer coated bread slice to the hot skillet over the butter.

4. Cook about two minutes per side, or until French toast is golden brown with dark brown edges. If you're using thick bread, gently sear each side edge of the toast (using clean tongs to hold the bread) until batter is cooked—maybe 15–30 seconds per side.

5. Continue the process with the rest of your slices, adding ½ teaspoon vegan butter to the pan before each slice.

6. Serve French toast warm and top with your preferred toppings.

pumpkin oat breakfast BREAD

Makes 1 (4×8-inch) loaf; serves 6–10

This breakfast bread isn't too sweet, so the Maple Hunny Butter really completes it. (Check out the photo on page 26 to see what I mean.) Slicing into it feels rustic, homey, and festive. Its complex flavors make it seem like it should be difficult and time consuming to make, but it's actually simple and so rewarding. It also makes a great housewarming gift if you've got new neighbors. Go say "hi"—you never know where your next great friendship may begin!

STUFF YOU NEED

1   cup cornmeal

1   cup all-purpose flour

⅔   cup cane sugar

2   tablespoons potato starch

1   teaspoon baking powder

1   teaspoon salt

½   teaspoon ground cinnamon

¼   teaspoon ground nutmeg

1   cup canned pumpkin puree

⅔   cup unsweetened non-dairy milk
     (rice milk recommended)

3   tablespoons maple syrup

2   tablespoons vegetable oil

1   teaspoon unsulphured molasses

1   teaspoon vanilla extract

⅛   teaspoon anise extract, optional

½   cup rolled oats, plus extra for topping

Toppings: pepitas and coarse-ground salt
For serving: Maple Hunny Butter (page 188)

WHAT TO DO

1. Preheat the oven to 350°F.

2. Combine all dry ingredients except oats in a large bowl and whisk together. Add all wet ingredients and mix well with a spatula. Break up all chunks, then stir in rolled oats.

3. Cut a sheet of parchment paper to fit the bottom of a 4×8-inch loaf dish (recommended), or spray the sides and bottom with nonstick baking spray.

4. Transfer batter to the prepared loaf dish and use your spatula to spread out evenly. Top with pepitas, oats, and salt. Bake for about 1 hour, or until the top of the loaf has cracked open and browned slightly.

5. When the loaf has cooled, flip the bread out of the pan, remove the parchment paper, and slice. Serve with homemade Maple Hunny Butter.

38   *The Cajun Vegan Cookbook*

strawberry peach **HEART TARTS**

Makes 12–15 tarts (depending on the size of your cookie cutter)

I never understood why Pop-Tarts were allowed to be breakfast, but pie was not. Aren't Pop-Tarts basically just little hand pies? Plump, delicious strawberries and peaches are both grown in Louisiana, and we're proud of them. After having Southern peaches, it's hard to want to eat other kinds. I used a 3½-inch-wide, heart-shaped cookie cutter to make these, but you can use any shape or size you want.

STUFF YOU NEED

Pastry

2½ cups all-purpose flour

2 tablespoons cane sugar

1 teaspoon salt

½ cup vegan butter, cold

½ cup vegetable shortening

¼ cup unsweetened non-dairy milk, chilled (rice milk recommended)

2 tablespoons water, chilled

Filling

1 cup diced peach (about 1 peach)

¼ cup water

1 tablespoon cane sugar

¼ teaspoon cornstarch

1 cup diced strawberries (about ½ pound)

Icing

1 cup powdered sugar

1½ tablespoons unsweetened non-dairy milk

¼ teaspoon vanilla extract

Optional: food coloring, sprinkles, and sugar for topping

Special tools: cookie cutter (I used a 3 ½-inch wide heart shape, but you can use any shape/size you want)

WHAT TO DO

1. Start with the pastry. In a medium bowl, whisk together flour, sugar, and salt.

2. Chop vegan butter and shortening into 1-inch chunks, then use a dough cutter or fork to cut butter and shortening into flour. Keep cutting until the dough resembles gravel.

3. Add non-dairy milk and chilled water. Use your hands to knead the dough until all ingredients are well combined and the dough resembles Play-Doh. Split dough into two equal balls. Wrap each ball in plastic wrap or place in a bowl and cover, and store in the fridge while you prepare your filling.

4. Heat a small pot over medium heat and add peaches, water, sugar, and cornstarch. Bring to a boil, then reduce heat to a gentle simmer. Cook for 10 minutes, then add strawberries and continue cooking for another 20 minutes, or until fruit has broken down and most of the liquid is gone. It should look a bit like roadkill, but taste delicious. Don't forget to scrape the bottom of the pot occasionally to avoid sticking and burning. Trust me...it can definitely burn. If you are a skilled multitasker, you can start the next step while the filling is cooking. Otherwise, just watch your strawberries and peaches! When filling is done, remove from heat and let cool completely.

5. Preheat your oven to 350°F and remove one of your dough balls from the fridge. On a floured surface, use a rolling pin to roll out the ball to ⅛ inch thick or less. The thinner it is, the better, without making it so thin that it falls apart! Lightly flour your rolling pin if your dough feels sticky.

(Recipe continues on next page)

(Recipe continued from previous page)

6. Use a cookie cutter to cut as many hearts (or whatever shape you're using) as you can out of the first dough ball, re-rolling after cutting out your first sheet. I got about 15 hearts total using my 3½-inch-wide heart cutter, just to give you a frame of reference. You could also use a knife or pastry wheel if you want to make rectangles, but it is kind of tricky to get the tops and bottoms to line up perfectly without the cookie cutter.

7. Transfer your shapes to a baking sheet (these will be your tart bottoms). If your filling hasn't finished cooking and cooling yet, throw your baking sheet in the fridge and wait. I recommend using this time to make your icing—just whisk all ingredients together, and add your food coloring of choice, if using. Beet powder makes a great natural food coloring, FYI!

8. Once your filling has finished cooking and cooling, scoop ½ tablespoon of filling onto each tart bottom. You may want to adjust this amount up or down depending upon how big your tarts are, but just leave ¼-inch to ½-inch of pastry bare around the edges for sealing.

9. Pull out the other dough ball from the fridge. Re-flour your surface and repeat the rolling and cutting process to form top pieces. Set top pieces over the filling, then use the prongs of a fork to press and seal the edges together. Finally, use the fork to poke the top of each tart 2–3 times to let out steam.

10. Bake for 30 minutes, or until edges are light golden brown. If you haven't already made your icing, use this time to do it. Or hey, just relax and enjoy the yummy smells! You'll need to wait for the pastries to cool anyway, so there will be time later for the icing, too.

11. Remove from the oven and allow tarts to cool completely before icing, or else you'll wind up with a drippy, melted mess. Spread a thin layer of icing over each tart using a mini spatula, or just drizzle them with icing. Sprinkle with sugar and sprinkles, if using, and enjoy fresh. These may also be frozen to keep longer! Allow to defrost at room temperature for at least 1 hour before enjoying.

FUN FACT To a botanist, strawberries are not actually fruits, and the "seeds" on the outside are not actually seeds—they are achenes. The achene is the true fruit, and inside each achene is a true seed. The red, delicious part of the strawberry is just the receptacle, and it grows to attract pollinators (a.k.a. bees).

backwoods buttermilk BISCUITS

The way a Southerner makes biscuits is like a thumbprint: no two are the same. But all of our versions lean heavily on the biscuit knowledge that came before us. We won't stray far from the original ingredients, and only make small tweaks here and there to make them ours.

STUFF YOU NEED

1¼ cups unsweetened non-dairy milk (rice milk recommended), plus extra as needed

2 teaspoons apple cider vinegar

3½ cups all-purpose flour

2 tablespoons cane sugar

2 tablespoons baking powder

½ teaspoon baking soda

1½ teaspoons salt

½ cup vegan butter, chilled, plus extra for brushing and greasing the pan

Recommended toppings: vegan butter, White Sausage Gravy (page 43), fruit jam, or maple syrup

Special tool: 2½-inch biscuit cutter. You could technically use a cup instead, but a biscuit cutter has much sharper edges and creates a clean cut. A dull cutter will smoosh the biscuit edges together, keeping the biscuits from rising properly.

Note: *Cutting in the cold butter creates butter "pockets" in the biscuit dough that will melt and steam during baking, creating flaky layers. You want your butter chilled because soft or melted butter will not form layers very well and will leave you with a tougher, flatter final product.

WHAT TO DO

1. Preheat the oven to 450°F.

2. In a small bowl, mix non-dairy milk and apple cider vinegar. Set aside.

3. In a separate medium bowl, whisk together all dry ingredients. Use a dough cutter or pastry blender (or a fork) to quickly cut in chilled butter until the butter is mostly broken up and resembles coarse, pebbly gravel.*

4. Add wet ingredients to your bowl of dry ingredients. Stir lightly with a spatula, then use your hands to gently knead the dough until all ingredients are just barely combined. The dough should be a little bit sticky. If it's not, add a few more splashes of non-dairy milk.

5. Flour a flat surface, then roll out the dough until it is ¾–1 inch thick. Use a 2½-inch biscuit cutter** to cut round discs. Be sure to cut straight down, then right back up (don't twist).

6. Grease a cast-iron skillet or baking pan with 1 tablespoon of vegan butter, then place biscuits next to each other in the pan, with their edges just barely touching to help them rise. Keep the biscuits away from the edges of the pan, if possible. Note: If you're using a smaller cast-iron skillet, you may have to break up the baking into two sessions in order to fit in all the biscuits. But yum...fresh seconds!

7. Brush the top of your biscuits with melted vegan butter, if desired, and bake for 18–25 minutes, or until the biscuit tops turn golden brown. Your baking time will depend on the type of pan used and your oven's gusto.

8. Serve with vegan butter, gravy, jam, or syrup and enjoy warm.

white sausage **GRAVY**

This is a quick and easy gravy, so whip it up while your biscuits are baking! For me, it's (almost) difficult to eat a biscuit without this gravy now because it's just that delicious. I try to mix things up by topping my biscuits with strawberry jam every now and again, but this gravy always calls me back to my roots.

STUFF YOU NEED

1½ cups unsweetened non-dairy milk
    (rice milk recommended)

½   cup vegan butter

3   tablespoons all-purpose flour

2   teaspoons freshly cracked
    black pepper

1   teaspoon salt

1   teaspoon garlic powder

1   teaspoon onion powder

1–2 links vegan sausage (Field Roast
    brand Apple Sage recommended),
    diced into ½-inch pieces

Toppings: fresh parsley

WHAT TO DO

1. Heat a 2-quart pot over medium heat. Add non-dairy milk and vegan butter and whisk together. Heat until butter is melted.

2. Whisk in flour, black pepper, salt, garlic powder, and onion powder. Gently boil until sauce thickens and browns slightly, 8–10 minutes. If you prefer a thinner or thicker sauce, adjust cook time accordingly. A longer cook time will make a thicker gravy, and cutting the cook time short will leave you with a thinner gravy. But be aware that the gravy will thicken slightly as it cools.

3. When gravy has reached the desired consistency, add vegan sausage, crumbling up chunks into smaller pieces with your hands before adding to the pot. (Big, hot dog–looking pieces of sausage are gross...you want it to look more like cooked ground beef in your gravy).

4. Serve warm over biscuits and top with fresh parsley.

Krimfession time: even though Southerners love to rave about how delicious fresh tomatoes are, I've never been much of a raw tomato person. I mean, I like ketchup...but otherwise, no thanks. I once watched someone eat a plain mayo and tomato sandwich on white bread, and they "yummmm"-ed the whole time. You can keep that mess. I do, however, love the deep, interesting flavor of sun-dried tomatoes. Are you into mushrooms? Throw in a package of sliced mushrooms with the onions and bell peppers for an extra somethin' somethin'. That, along with the sweet potatoes, is what makes this one of my favorite breakfast dishes.

STUFF YOU NEED

2　tablespoons olive oil, plus extra as needed

3　cups chopped russet potatoes (skin on, ½-inch pieces; about 2 medium potatoes)

2　cups chopped sweet potatoes (skin on, ½-inch pieces; about 1 medium potato)

1　cup diced white onion (about ½ large onion)

½　cup diced red bell pepper (about ½ small pepper)

½　cup diced green bell pepper (about ½ small pepper)

½　cup finely diced sun-dried tomatoes (jarred in oil)

1　tablespoon minced garlic

2　teaspoons Krimsey's Cajun Seasoning (page 193)

½　teaspoon salt, or to taste

Recommended toppings: chopped fresh parsley, freshly cracked black pepper, and Smoky Maple Bacon Bits (page 196).

WHAT TO DO

1. Heat olive oil over medium heat in a cast-iron skillet (or another large skillet) with a lid. If you're using cast iron, don't forget to preheat your pan for 10 minutes prior to cooking. Then, watch your heat. You may need to turn things down a bit if the oil is popping and sizzling out of the pan.

2. Add russet and sweet potatoes, stir to coat, and cook, covered, for 5–7 minutes, or until potatoes begin to get a little tender and some edges start to brown. Stir once every 2–3 minutes. If things are sticking terribly, add another tablespoon of olive oil.

3. Once potatoes are slightly softened, add onion, bell peppers, and sun-dried tomatoes. Cook uncovered for 10–15 minutes, stirring every minute or so until veggies are tender and potatoes can be easily pierced with a fork.

4. Add garlic, Cajun seasoning, and salt. Mix and cook for another 3–4 minutes, or until garlic is fragrant. By now, your potatoes should be completely cooked through. If not, let them go a couple of minutes longer.

5. Allow to cool slightly, then top with fresh parsley, black pepper, and/or Smoky Maple Bacon Bits. Don't burn your mouth, my friend.

TIP
Try subbing in different kinds of potatoes for this hash! Waxier potatoes (like red potatoes, fingerlings, or Yukon golds) will hold their shape a bit better due to a lower starch content, if that's your style. But I love starch, so gimme those russets.

spicy cajun sausage FRITTATA

Makes 1 (10-inch) frittata; serves 8–12 **GF**

At the time of this book writing, there are only a few suppliers of vegan egg products. For this recipe, I used powdered VeganEgg by Follow Your Heart. There is also a JUST Egg plant-based scramble that comes ready-made and pourable. (If you opt for this brand, omit water and milk from recipe and instead just use 24 ounces of JUST Egg since it's already liquid.) If you don't have access to a vegan egg product, I don't recommend attempting this recipe. The egg powder is the main binder for this recipe, and it gives it that savory "eggy" taste. I use a cast-iron skillet for this recipe, but you could also sub in a cake pan or oven-safe skillet. The cast iron does a good job of cooking things evenly all around and holding heat after cooking, though. Plus, it's much more impressive looking if you want to feel like an all-star Southern chef.

STUFF YOU NEED

- 1 teaspoon vegetable oil
- 2 vegan sausages (spicy recommended), diced
- 1 (4-ounce) package powdered VeganEgg
- 1 teaspoon Krimsey's Cajun Seasoning (page 193)
- 1 teaspoon freshly cracked black pepper
- ½ teaspoon salt
- 2 cups water
- 1½ cups unsweetened non-dairy milk
- 1 cup vegan cheddar cheese shreds
- ½ small white onion, thinly sliced
- ½ medium red bell pepper, sliced into 2-inch-long, ¼-inch-wide strips
- 2 tablespoons sliced green onions
- 2 teaspoons minced garlic
- 1 tablespoon vegan butter

Toppings: hot sauce and fresh cilantro or parsley

WHAT TO DO

1. Preheat the oven to 350°F. Put your cast-iron skillet in the oven to heat up while you prepare your ingredients.

2. Heat oil in a small pot or skillet over medium heat. Add vegan sausage and sauté for 5–6 minutes, or until slightly browned. Set aside.

3. In a medium bowl, whisk together VeganEgg powder, Cajun seasoning, black pepper, and salt. Add water and non-dairy milk and use a spatula to blend well.

4. Mix in vegan cheddar cheese, onion, red bell pepper, green onion, garlic, and vegan sausage.

5. Once the oven is preheated, carefully remove the cast-iron skillet from the oven and add vegan butter. Tilt and rock the pan to distribute the melted butter, then pour in your Vegan Egg mixture. Use your spatula to spread out the mixture evenly in the pan.

6. Bake for about 45 minutes, or until eggs are set and the top begins to darken slightly.

7. Allow to cool for 10 minutes, then slice and serve warm! When it's time to serve, top with hot sauce and fresh cilantro or parsley.

Krimfession Time...

One time I accidentally used cilantro here (when I meant to use parsley) and discovered that I like the punch of cilantro better on this dish! They look very similar...it could happen to anyone. At least that's what I tell myself when I make goofs like this.

savory steel-cut cajun OATMEAL

Savory oatmeal is new to me, but I love it, and I love sharing it with others. Squint your mind a bit and think of it kind of like grits. My favorite recipe is below, but because most of the items are toppings, you can swap and omit ingredients to fit your personal style. Here's a fun, useless fact: I've been eating oatmeal nearly every morning for over two years now! I love it. Hearty, predictable, and simple. Just like potatoes, my other favorite food.

STUFF YOU NEED

3   cups water

1   cup unsweetened non-dairy milk
    (rice milk recommended)

½   teaspoon salt

½   teaspoon freshly cracked
    black pepper

1   cup steel-cut oats (not quick-cook;
    use gluten-free if desired)

4   ounces tempeh

2   teaspoons olive oil

1   tablespoon soy sauce (or gluten-free
    soy sauce or tamari)

2   tablespoons raw pine nuts

Recommended toppings: arugula, avocado, halved cherry tomatoes, basil, Krimsey's Cajun Seasoning (page 193), and hot sauce

WHAT TO DO

1. In a 3-quart pot, bring water, non-dairy milk, salt, and black pepper to a low boil. Add oats and adjust temperature so that the mixture is simmering lightly. Don't walk away from the pot until everything is stabilized—oatmeal loves to boil over when you're not looking!

2. Simmer gently, uncovered, for 30 minutes, or until oats are cooked through. Scrape the bottom of the pot periodically, especially during the last 5–10 minutes of cooking. The oatmeal should be thick and creamy when finished.

3. While oats are cooking, slice tempeh into ⅓-inch-thick strips (you should get about 6 strips) and prepare your preferred toppings.

4. Heat oil in a small frying pan over medium heat. When hot, add tempeh strips. Cook 4 minutes per side, or until golden brown. After both sides are cooked, lower heat and drizzle soy sauce over the strips. Flip and stir until all liquid has been absorbed. Set aside in a warm place.

5. Toast pine nuts in a small, dry saucepan over medium heat, stirring constantly (or shaking your pan) until pine nuts are spotted light golden brown. This should take 2–3 minutes total. Remove from the heat and continue stirring for another minute, until the pan has cooled down a bit.

6. When oatmeal is finished, portion out into 2 bowls and top with tempeh, pine nuts, and other preferred toppings.

Krimfession Time...

I never cook my oatmeal over the stove anymore. I now use a special pressurized oatmeal cooker (kind of like a rice cooker) so I can "set it and forget it" every morning.

Unbelievably savory, offensively quick, and undeniably interesting. This was a head turner at my restaurant, but adventurous eaters always licked their bowls clean.

STUFF YOU NEED

4   cups no-chicken broth (or vegetable stock)

1   cup quick-cooking grits

1   teaspoon olive oil

3   garlic cloves, minced

1   cup corn kernels (fresh or frozen)

1   teaspoon Krimsey's Cajun Seasoning (page 193)

½   teaspoon salt, or to taste

1   large handful spinach

Topping: freshly cracked black pepper

WHAT TO DO

1. Bring broth to a boil in a 4-quart pot over medium heat.

2. Add grits, reduce heat to medium-low, and simmer, stirring occasionally, for 7–10 minutes, or until grits are thick and look like molten lava.

3. While the grits are cooking, heat olive oil in a skillet over medium-high heat. Add garlic and cook until it starts to brown, 1–2 minutes.

4. Throw in corn, Cajun seasoning, and salt, then once the mixture is hot, add spinach. Allow spinach to wilt for about 1 minute, stirring often.

5. Once heated throughout, transfer cooked grits to serving bowls, then top with the spinach and corn mixture. Serve topped with freshly cracked black pepper.

Krimfession Time...

I always add vegan butter to grits. Am I a butter lush?

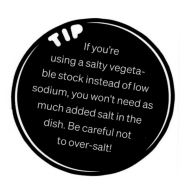

TIP If you're using a salty vegetable stock instead of low sodium, you won't need as much added salt in the dish. Be careful not to over-salt!

sourdough cinnamon ROLLS WITH CREAM CHEESE ICING *Makes 12 rolls*

As a kid, I loved making those "biscuits in a can" from the refrigerated section at the grocery store. Now that I'm older, I would probably still make those if they had a vegan version. Since they don't (yet), I've been pleasantly forced into making my own biscuits and cinnamon rolls, which I love even more.

STUFF YOU NEED

Dough

- 1 cup unsweetened non-dairy milk (rice milk recommended)
- ¾ cup vegan butter, melted
- ⅓ cup cane sugar
- 1 tablespoon baking powder
- 2¼ teaspoons instant active dry yeast (standard ¼-ounce packet)
- 1½ teaspoons salt
- 1 teaspoon vanilla extract
- ½ teaspoon ground nutmeg
- 3½ cups all-purpose flour (leveled off, not packed)

Filling

- 1½ tablespoons vegan butter, melted
- 2 teaspoons unsulphured molasses
- 2 teaspoons ground cinnamon
- ¾ cup light brown sugar

Icing

- 1½ cups powdered sugar
- ½ cup (4 ounces) vegan cream cheese, softened at room temperature
- ⅓ cup vegan butter, softened at room temperature
- 2 teaspoons fresh lemon juice

Optional: 1-3 teaspoons of non-dairy milk, if you like a thinner icing

WHAT TO DO

1. Start with making your dough. In a medium bowl, whisk together non-dairy milk and melted vegan butter, then add sugar, baking powder, yeast, salt, vanilla extract, and nutmeg.

2. Add flour 1 cup at a time, stirring with a large spoon as you go. Keep adding flour until the dough becomes too sticky to stir, then move to a lightly floured countertop surface and continue kneading by hand for 1 minute. When finished, the dough should form a light, smooshy ball. Be careful not to over-knead! It will make your dough tough.

3. Return dough to the bowl and cover with plastic wrap or a thin, lightly moistened cotton towel. Let rise for 1 hour in a warm place (ideally about 80°F), or until the dough has roughly doubled in size. But don't leave it somewhere too hot, or it will get crusty and dry.

4. Preheat your oven to 350°F.

5. After your dough has risen, move the fluffy ball to a lightly floured surface and roll out with a rolling pin to a ¼-inch-thick rectangle. (Mine was about 11×23 inches. Don't worry if your rectangle shape isn't perfect; it's still going to taste amazing.)

6. In a small bowl, mix vegan butter, molasses, and cinnamon together for your filling. Use a spatula to spread it out over the dough rectangle, then sprinkle brown sugar on top. Smooth that out with your spatula as well.

7. Beginning on one of the long edges, roll up your dough semi-tightly (but not stressfully) until you reach the opposite edge. Pinch edges to seal along the roll and place seal-side down.

(Recipe continues on next page)

(Recipe continued from previous page)

8. Using a serrated knife, cut 1½–2-inch-wide rolls from the dough log and place them cut side down on an oiled or parchment paper-lined baking sheet.

9. Bake for 30 minutes, or until golden brown.

10. While the cinnamon rolls are baking, prepare your cream cheese icing by beating together all icing ingredients with an electric mixer fitted with the whisk attachment, or using human power with a handheld whisk. You can make your icing thinner by adding a tiny bit of rice milk, if desired.

11. When rolls are done baking, remove from the oven and allow them to cool for 5–10 minutes before topping with icing and serving. Best enjoyed fresh!

TIP If you don't have access to vegan cream cheese, just use the icing recipe from Cinnamon King Cake, page 221.

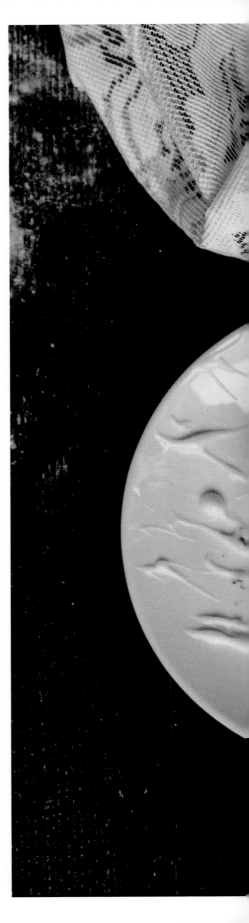

Jambalaya Soup

soups, salads,
& POBOYS

crabby palm & chickpea SALAD

Serves 2 (makes 2½ cups)

This is one of my favorite recipes in this book. My Granny always had tuna fish sandwiches ready for me when I came to visit her house. Kind of a weird grandma treat, but it's what I loved. This recipe reminds me of the yummy sandwiches I used to gorge on as a kid, but this salad has more of a Gulf Coast feel (and is obviously vegan). It's delicious, filling, and works super well in a sandwich. It's also great as a salad topping or in lettuce wraps.

STUFF YOU NEED

- 1½ cups cooked chickpeas
  (or one 15-ounce can, drained)
- 1 (15-ounce) can whole hearts of palm
- ½ cup finely diced celery
  (about 1 large stalk)
- ¼ cup finely diced white onion
  (about ¼ small onion)
- ½ cup finely diced green bell pepper
- ½ cup vegan mayo
- ¼ (8×8-inch) sheet dried roasted
  nori seaweed paper, crumbled
- 1 tablespoon olive oil
- 1 tablespoon Dijon mustard
- 1 teaspoon fresh parsley
- 1 teaspoon paprika
- 1 teaspoon celery salt
- 1 teaspoon freshly cracked
  black pepper
- ⅛ teaspoon ground mace
- ⅛ teaspoon cayenne pepper, optional
  (omit if you don't appreciate a
  little kick)
- Pinch of bay leaf powder

Toppings: fresh parsley and freshly cracked black pepper

WHAT TO DO

1. In a medium bowl, smash chickpeas with a fork.

2. Slice hearts of palm lengthwise, then chop into ½-inch crescents. Add hearts of palm to chickpeas and smash a bit more until the palm starts to look a little raggedy.

3. Mix in celery and onion, then add all other remaining ingredients and mix well using a large spoon or spatula.

4. Cover and chill in the refrigerator for at least 30 minutes before serving. If making ahead, store in refrigerator for up to a week. Top with fresh parsley and freshly cracked black pepper.

Soups, Salads, & Poboys   55

"oh susanna" **SALAD**

My friend Susanna originally shared this recipe with me, and with her permission, I gave it my own twist and am now sharing it with you. It's crispy and crunchy with just a touch of sweetness from the apples.

STUFF YOU NEED

- 2 stalks celery, diced into ½-inch pieces
- 2 apples, diced into ½-inch pieces (Gala or Honeycrisp recommended)
- 1½ cups cooked chickpeas (or one 15-ounce can, drained)
- 4 green onions, finely sliced on an angle
- ½ cup vegan mayo
- 1 teaspoon fresh lime juice
- 1 teaspoon fresh lemon juice
- 1 teaspoon apple cider vinegar
- ½ teaspoon salt
- ¼ teaspoon freshly cracked black pepper
- 1 cup cooked quinoa, chilled

Recommended toppings: avocado and freshly cracked black pepper

WHAT TO DO

1. Toss celery and apples together with chickpeas in a large bowl. Add green onions to the bowl and set aside.

2. In a smaller separate bowl, whisk together vegan mayo, lime juice, lemon juice, apple cider vinegar, salt, and black pepper.

3. Use a spatula to transfer mayo mixture to the bowl of diced celery, apples, and chickpeas. Stir well to coat, then add your cooked, chilled quinoa and mix again until distributed throughout.

4. Refrigerate for at least 30 minutes before serving. If making ahead, store in refrigerator for up to 3 days. Top with avocado and fresh-cracked black pepper, if desired.

TIP

To me, the main appeal of a salad is that I don't have to cook it. If that's you too, use frozen pre-cooked quinoa. Or hey, even better—cook it in bulk yourself and freeze it in small batches for future use.

cajun rainbow SALAD

Serves 1 **GF**

When you think of Cajun cuisine, your mind probably doesn't immediately conjure heaping bowls overflowing with leafy greens. Let's be honest, mine doesn't always either—but sometimes you just want something fresh and delicious. This salad was on the menu at my restaurant to provide a whole-food option for any wandering Cajuns looking for a healthy rainbow to eat. With Cajun Ranch, of course.

STUFF YOU NEED

1   big handful shredded curly kale
    (about 2½ ounces)

1   big handful baby spinach leaves
    (about 4 ounces)

¼   cup cooked and chilled kidney beans

¼   cup diced red bell pepper

¼   cup shredded carrots

¼   cup fresh corn kernels

5–6 cucumber slices, cut into
    half-moon shapes

¼   cup shredded red cabbage

¼   cup chopped canned hearts of palm

    Cajun Ranch (page 181)

Toppings: sliced green onions and Krimsey's Cajun Seasoning (page193)

WHAT TO DO

1. Layer kale and spinach at the bottom of your bowl. Arrange kidney beans, red bell pepper, carrots, corn, cucumber slices, red cabbage, and hearts of palm in a rainbow circle over the greens. *Hint for anyone who's forgotten the rainbow color order: the ingredients are already listed in order!*

2. Top with Cajun Ranch, then add Cajun seasoning and sliced green onions to taste. Enjoy this heart-healthy meal.

broiled palm poboy **SALAD**

This salad is a whole-food alternative to the New Orleans Palm Poboy. If you want to stay ultra-true to the taste and feel of a Palm Poboy, use fried palm (see page 119; about ¼ batch will be sufficient for this salad). Prepare the fried palm nuggets after you've assembled your salad base. Or if you want to keep things on the healthier side, broil your hearts of palm as instructed below.

STUFF YOU NEED

- ½   cup chopped hearts of palm (about 2 stalks from a can), sliced lengthwise and then cut into 1/8-inch slices
- 1   teaspoon vegetable oil, divided
- ½   teaspoon paprika
  Pinch of salt
- ⅓   cup corn kernels, fresh or frozen
- ¼   teaspoon Krimsey's Cajun Seasoning (page 193), plus extra for topping
- 1   small handful shredded curly kale
- 1   small handful baby spinach leaves
- ¼   cup shredded iceberg lettuce
- ½   cup shredded carrots
- ¼   cup diced tomatoes
- 2   tablespoons diced red cabbage
- 1   sliced avocado
  Cajun Ranch (page 181)

WHAT TO DO

1. Preheat your oven to broil.

2. In the smallest baking pan you have, drizzle hearts of palm with ½ teaspoon of vegetable oil. Broil on the middle rack of your oven for 8 minutes. Remove from the oven, sprinkle with paprika and salt, and stir before returning to the oven for another 6 minutes. Set aside.

3. Next, make your blackened Cajun corn. In a small skillet, heat remaining ½ teaspoon vegetable oil over medium heat. Add corn, spread out into a single layer, and cook for about 4 minutes, only stirring once per minute. When done, the corn should have some golden-brownish pieces. Sprinkle Cajun seasoning on the corn and mix well. Raise heat to medium-high, cover, and cook stirring only once at the halfway mark, for another 2 minutes or until some blackened edges start showing up. You'll want to cover the pan simply to keep the corn from popping all over your kitchen (yep, it happens!). When finished, set aside to cool.

4. Layer kale, spinach, and iceberg lettuce at the bottom of your bowl. Spread carrots, tomatoes, red cabbage, sliced avocado, blackened corn, and broiled hearts of palm on top of your greens.

5. Serve with a sprinkle of Cajun seasoning and Cajun Ranch dressing.

southern belle pepper SALAD

The name of this dish is a defiant act of reclamation, because the term "Southern Belle" is—to be charitable—restrictive. To be less patronizing, it's gross and severely outdated and makes me throw up in my mouth a little bit. It fills my soul to see women and girls being confident, free, loud, and undaunted by the limited imaginations and opinions of others. Boldness, personality, and inclusivity make everything better, which is why all the bell peppers in the rainbow are added to this salad (except green ones—they're just unripe red peppers and they're kind of bitter when raw). The spice and tang of the peppers embody this irreverent outlook, making you perk up and pay attention.

STUFF YOU NEED

2   handfuls spring mix lettuce
     (about 2½ ounces)

¼   medium red bell pepper

¼   medium orange bell pepper

¼   medium yellow bell pepper

3–4 baby purple carrots, diced
     (or ½ regular purple carrot)

¼   cup cooked chickpeas

¼   cup Roasted & Salted Pecans
     (page 197)

1   sprig fresh basil, for garnish

     Pinch of coarse-ground salt

     Pinch of freshly cracked black pepper

     Tangy Tabasco Dressing (page 177)

WHAT TO DO

1. Create a fluffy bed of spring mix in your serving bowl.

2. If you like to play with your food, like I do, slice your bell peppers in a way that feels fun to you and make some art. Add peppers to spring mix, then top with all remaining ingredients. For a still delicious but less photogenic salad, dice bell peppers and toss together with spring mix, carrots, chickpeas, pecans, salt, pepper, and basil. Top with Tangy Tabasco Dressing.

tchoupitoulas SALAD

Serves 1 **GF**

Pronounced "CHOP-ah-too-lus," Tchoupitoulas Street was named after the Native American tribe côte de Chapitoulas, meaning "those who live by the river." Running along the Mississippi River in uptown New Orleans, it's home to many famous restaurants, hotels, and other historic attractions. We served this salad at the restaurant because it's fresh, crunchy, and delicious...and maybe also because listening to customers trying to pronounce it made me smile.

STUFF YOU NEED

1   teaspoon olive oil

½   cup corn kernels, fresh or frozen

¼   teaspoon Krimsey's Cajun Seasoning (page 193), plus extra for topping

1   big handful shredded curly kale (about 2½ ounces)

1   big handful baby spinach leaves (about 4 ounces)

⅓   cup cooked and chilled black-eyed peas

¼   cup diced red cabbage

¼   cup Roasted & Salted Pecans (page 197)

1   tablespoon Smoky Maple Bacon Bits (page 196)

    Hunny Mustard (page 192)

WHAT TO DO

1. Make your blackened Cajun corn. In a small skillet, heat olive oil over medium heat. Add corn, spread out into a single layer, and cook for about 4 minutes, only stirring once per minute. When done, the corn should have some golden brownish pieces. Sprinkle Cajun seasoning on the corn and mix well. Raise heat to medium-high, cover, and cook, stirring only once at the halfway mark, for another 2 minutes or until some blackened edges start showing up. You'll want to cover the pan simply to keep the corn from popping all over your kitchen (yep, it happens!). When finished, set aside to cool.

2. Layer kale and spinach at the bottom of your bowl, then arrange black-eyed peas, red cabbage, pecans, and blackened corn on top.

3. Top with Smoky Maple Bacon Bits and a sprinkle of Cajun seasoning.

4. Serve with Hunny Mustard dressing.

cajun caesar **SALAD**

Serves 1

I used to love Caesar salad for its tangy qualities and spicy flavor. Later, I realized that the tangy, tongue-tickling spiciness in the Caesar dressing was due to the anchovies in it. Little smelly hidden fishies in my salad. Oops. So, I created my own fish-free version of this popular salad, this time with some Southern flair (of course).

STUFF YOU NEED

1 whole head romaine lettuce, chopped into 1-inch strips

½ cup Garlic Sourdough Croutons (page 195)

½ cup diced red bell pepper

½ cup vegan mozzarella cheese shreds

½ teaspoon freshly cracked black pepper

Cajun Caesar Dressing (page 174)

Toppings: vegan parmesan cheese crumbles, freshly cracked black pepper, and lemon wedges

WHAT TO DO

1. In a large bowl, toss romaine strips, croutons, red bell pepper, vegan mozzarella, and black pepper together.

2. If serving salad immediately, pour dressing over romaine mixture in stages, mixing with tongs as you go to achieve desired coverage. I usually recommend 3–4 tablespoons per batch, but I've been known to go heavier at times.

3. Garnish with vegan parmesan cheese, freshly cracked black pepper, and lemon wedges. And maybe some more croutons, am I right?

corn & baked potato CHOWDER

Serves 4–6 (makes about 2 quarts) **GF**

Originally created to be a seasonal winter dish, I quickly realized that this was a recipe worth making year-round. The chunky baked potato flavor, combined with the Smoky Maple Bacon Bits, make this a homey, comforting dish that's hard to put down.

STUFF YOU NEED

- 3 medium russet potatoes (about 1 pound each)
- 2 teaspoons olive oil
- 3 stalks celery, diced
- 1 small white onion, diced
- 1 tablespoon minced garlic
- 4 cups low-sodium vegetable stock
- 2½ cups unsweetened non-dairy milk (rice milk recommended)
- 4 cups corn kernels, fresh or frozen
- 2 teaspoons salt, or to taste
- 1½ teaspoons freshly cracked black pepper
- 1½ teaspoons garlic powder
- 1½ teaspoons onion powder
- ½ teaspoon white pepper
- ¼ teaspoon liquid smoke
- 2 teaspoons fresh thyme leaves

Toppings: sliced green onions and Smoky Maple Bacon Bits (page 196)

WHAT TO DO

1. Preheat your oven to 375°F.

2. Wash and scrub all the potatoes, leaving the skins on. Slice potatoes in half lengthwise so that you wind up with potato "hills" that have flat bottoms.

3. Place potatoes cut side down on a lightly oiled baking sheet and bake on the middle oven rack for 30–35 minutes, or until you're able to poke a fork through them. Let cool for about 10 minutes, then chop into 1-inch pieces.

4. Heat olive oil in a 4-quart pot over medium heat. Add celery and onion and sauté for 5 minutes. Add garlic and cook for another 2 minutes, stirring occasionally.

5. Add vegetable stock, non-dairy milk, corn, salt, black pepper, garlic powder, onion powder, white pepper, and liquid smoke. (Save the thyme for later.) If your potatoes are ready, go ahead and bring the liquids to a simmer. If not, wait for the potatoes to finish cooking.

6. Once chowder is simmering, add potato chunks and cook for 12–15 minutes, or until the soup thickens a bit and all flavors are incorporated.

7. When it's done, remove from the heat and toss in the thyme. Use a potato masher or sturdy spoon to smoosh up some of the potatoes until the soup is a consistency that you like. Salt to taste, and top with sliced green onions and Smoky Maple Bacon Bits.

cajun slow cooker **WHITE BEAN SOUP**

Serves 8–12 (makes about 4 quarts) **GF**

I like the simplicity of throwing everything together in a slow cooker in the morning, then having dinner all ready to go later. If you don't want to use a slow cooker, you can also just follow the same flow and replace the slow cooker time with about 2½ hours simmering time on the stovetop. You may need to add an extra cup of water or two if using the stovetop, though, since you'll have more liquid boiling off during cooking. If you'd rather go the whole foods route, swap out the sausage for some kale or other greens!

STUFF YOU NEED

1   pound dried white navy beans (or Great Northern beans)

4   cups low-sodium vegetable stock

3   cups water

2   cups sliced celery, sliced lengthwise into ⅓-inch-thick slices (about 3 large stalks)

2   cups sliced carrots, sliced on a bias to make ⅓-inch-thick "chips" (about ½ pound)

1   (15-ounce) can fire-roasted diced tomatoes, with juice

2   teaspoons Krimsey's Cajun Seasoning (page 193)

1   teaspoon garlic powder

2   bay leaves

1½ teaspoons salt, or to taste

1   teaspoon freshly cracked black pepper

1   tablespoon olive oil

4   links vegan sausage (Andouille or spicy flavor), cut into ⅓-inch slices on a bias (omit if making gluten-free)

2   tablespoons tightly packed chopped fresh parsley

For serving: hot sauce and French bread

WHAT TO DO

1. Rinse and drain your beans, then transfer to a 4-quart slow cooker.

2. Add vegetable stock, water, celery, carrots, diced tomatoes, Cajun seasoning, garlic powder, bay leaves, salt, and black pepper.

3. Cook for 6–8 hours on low heat, or about 4 hours on high heat (cook times will vary depending on the strength of your cooker).

4. Just before soup is done, heat olive oil in a large pan over medium-high heat. Add vegan sausage slices and sauté until sausage is slightly browned with blackened edges, 6–8 minutes. Stir and flip often. This is a time where you should err on the side of "overcooked," because the sausage will soften up after you add it to the soup.

5. When soup is done cooking, use a large spoon or potato masher to smoosh up about 1 cup worth of beans. This will thicken the soup a bit.

6. Just before serving, add sausage to the soup. Taste and add more salt and spices as desired. Add chopped parsley and serve with hot sauce and French bread.

louisiana GUMBO

Gumbo: one of Louisiana's most recognizable dishes. Like all of the best regional cuisine (if done well), the taste can transport you. There are tons of versions and variations of gumbo, but this particular recipe builds on Cajun traditions, of course. Creole gumbos, for example, usually contain tomatoes. If you don't like okra, don't freak out. Just leave it out and sub in some of the optional add-ins at the bottom of the ingredients list. The most important thing to remember about this dish? Don't rush it. Enjoy the ride. For a fun variation, use jambalaya instead of parboiled rice to make a combo "Gumbalaya" dish!

STUFF YOU NEED

½ cup vegetable oil

½ cup all-purpose flour (for gluten-free, use ¼ cup rice flour instead)

1 cup chopped white onion (about ½ large onion)

1 cup chopped green bell pepper (about 1 small bell pepper)

1 cup diced celery (about 2 stalks)

2 teaspoons minced garlic

4 cups water

2 Not-Chick'n bouillon cubes (or use low-sodium vegetable stock instead of water and bouillon)

2 teaspoons Krimsey's Cajun Seasoning (page 193)

2 teaspoons apple cider vinegar

2 teaspoons gumbo filé powder

1 teaspoon unsulphured molasses

½ teaspoon dried thyme

(Ingredients continue on next page)

WHAT TO DO

1. To start your roux, heat oil in a 4-quart (or larger) pot over medium-low heat. Slowly add flour and use a flat-bottomed spoon to stir continuously. Be careful not to splash yourself—it's easy to do if you're not careful.

2. Keep stirring! It is extremely important that you do not walk away from the pot. The phases of colors for your roux will go something like this: peanut butter, pumpkin puree, milk chocolate. Keep stirring until it is just barely the color of milk chocolate, about 15 minutes.

3. Quickly add onion, bell pepper, and celery to cool down the roux. Stir to coat and cook for 5 minutes, then add garlic and cook for another 2 minutes.

4. Add water, bouillon cubes, Cajun seasoning, apple cider vinegar, gumbo filé powder, molasses, thyme, black pepper, and bay leaf and bring to a gentle simmer. Once bubbling, add okra, black-eyed peas, and kidney beans. Use your hands to crush up hearts of palm pieces before dropping into the gumbo—it should start to look a bit like shredded crab meat. Add any optional add-ins, too.

(Recipe continues on next page)

TIP

The roux (pronounced "roo") is an extremely important part of Cajun cooking, and it's important not to rush this step. If you burn it, you gotta start over!

(Recipe & ingredients continued from previous page)

½ teaspoon freshly cracked black pepper

⅛ teaspoon ground bay leaf (or 1 whole bay leaf)

2 cups frozen okra

1½ cups cooked black-eyed peas (or one 15-ounce can)

1½ cups cooked kidney beans (or one 15-ounce can)

½ can whole hearts of palm, drained and chopped into 1-inch-thick rounds (7 ounces)

Toppings: cooked rice, fresh parsley, and sliced green onions

Optional add-ins: roasted cauliflower, vegan sausage, mushrooms (try oyster or lion's mane), vegan chicken, black beans

5. Continue cooking for about 15 minutes, or until all veggies are tender. If you like a thinner gumbo, add more water ½ cup at a time until it suits you.

6. Transfer to serving bowls and top with cooked rice, sliced green onions, and fresh parsley.

Krimfession Time...

I'm impatient when it comes to making a roux, so I "cheat" by turning up the heat to medium or medium-high during the first part of cooking. Once the roux shows the first signs of browning (turning a light peanut butter color), I immediately turn the heat back down to medium-low.

jambalaya SOUP

eavesServes 6–10 (makes about 3 quarts)

This recipe (pictured on page 52) is great for dinner parties because you can pre-chop everything, then just let the aroma fill the house as you casually stir your concoction like a calm and collected kitchen witch. Be sure to pre-chop all your veggies and the sausage; otherwise, you may find yourself feeling stressed by the timing of this recipe. Recommended: Serve this soup with cornbread!

STUFF YOU NEED

3   tablespoons vegetable oil, divided

1½ cups chopped celery
     (2–3 medium stalks)

1½ cups chopped yellow bell pepper
     (about 1 medium pepper)

1½ cups chopped yellow onion
     (about 1 large onion)

1½ tablespoons minced garlic

5   cups low-sodium vegetable stock

2½ cups water

1   cup dry parboiled rice

1   (14-ounce) can diced fire-roasted
     tomatoes, with juice

2½ teaspoons Krimsey's Cajun
     Seasoning (page 193)

1½ teaspoons salt

⅛   teaspoon ground bay leaf
     (or 1 whole bay leaf)

4   links vegan sausage (Andouille or
     spicy flavor), halved lengthwise and
     sliced into half-moon shapes

1½ cups cooked kidney beans
     (about one 15-ounce can)

1½ cups cooked black-eyed peas
     (about one 15-ounce can)

Toppings: fresh parsley and fresh thyme

WHAT TO DO

1. Heat 2 tablespoons vegetable oil in a 6-quart (or larger) pot over medium heat.

2. When oil is hot, add celery, yellow bell pepper, and onion. Sauté for 4 minutes, or until veggies begin to soften slightly, then add garlic and cook, stirring periodically, for 2 more minutes.

3. Add vegetable stock, water, rice, tomatoes with their juice, Cajun seasoning, salt, and bay leaf. Once the liquids begin simmering, cover and cook for 10 minutes. When finished, the rice should be semi-cooked but still a bit crunchy.

4. While your soup is simmering, heat remaining 1 tablespoon vegetable oil in a large skillet over medium-high heat. Add vegan sausage slices and sauté until the edges are slightly browned, about 5 minutes. Set aside.

5. When the soup has simmered for 10 minutes, toss in kidney beans, black-eyed peas, and vegan sausage. Simmer gently for another 5–10 minutes, or until rice is cooked through without being mushy. Note: If you find that your liquid is boiling off too quickly, just add a touch more veggie broth or water (⅓ cup at a time) to make it soupier.

6. Portion into serving bowls, top with fresh parsley and thyme, and enjoy!

TIP This is a dish best served fresh, because the rice will continue to soak up liquids over time. However, you can remedy that by simply adding more veggie broth or water when reheating. Or just enjoy it as jambalaya (no soup) the next day!

green gumbo **("GUMBO Z'HERBS")**

Serves 4–6 (makes about 2 quarts) **GF**

"Green Gumbo" is a traditional Lenten dish in Louisiana, often served on Good Friday. The tradition is to add many greens, for every green you add means a new friend in the coming year. This special gumbo was likely influenced by a few other similar dishes from around the world, including Callaloo, from Africa, Potage aux Herbes from France, and Green Thursday Soup from Germany.

STUFF YOU NEED

½   cup vegetable oil

½   cup all-purpose flour (for gluten-free, use ¼ cup rice flour instead)

1   cup diced white onion (about ½ large onion)

1   cup diced green bell pepper (about 1 small bell pepper)

1   cup chopped celery (about 2 stalks)

2   teaspoons minced garlic

5   cups water

2   Not-Chick'n bouillon cubes (or use low-sodium vegetable stock instead of water and bouillon)

2   teaspoons apple cider vinegar

1½ teaspoons Krimsey's Cajun Seasoning (page 193)

1½ teaspoons gumbo filé powder

1   teaspoon unsulphured molasses

½   teaspoon dried thyme

½   teaspoon salt

½   teaspoon freshly cracked black pepper

⅛   teaspoon ground bay leaf (or 1 whole bay leaf)

4   large dinosaur kale leaves, chopped

2   large mustard green leaves, chopped

2   large swiss chard leaves, chopped

2   large turnip green leaves, chopped

2   large collard green leaves, chopped

Toppings: cooked rice, fresh parsley, and sliced green onions

WHAT TO DO

1. To make your roux, heat oil in a 4-quart (or larger) pot over medium-low heat, then slowly add flour. Use a flat-bottomed spoon to stir continuously. Be careful not to splash yourself—it's easy to do if you're not careful.

2. Keep stirring! It is extremely important that you do not walk away from the pot. The phases of colors for your roux will go something like this: peanut butter, pumpkin puree, milk chocolate. Keep stirring until it is just barely the color of milk chocolate, about 15 minutes.

3. Quickly add onion, bell pepper, and celery to cool down the roux. Stir to coat and cook for 5 minutes, then add garlic and cook for another 2 minutes.

4. Add water, bouillon cubes, apple cider vinegar, Cajun seasoning, gumbo filé powder, molasses, thyme, salt, pepper, and bay leaf. Bring to a gentle simmer, then add chopped greens. Cook for about 15 minutes, or until greens are tender. If you like a thinner gumbo, add more water ½ cup at a time until it suits you.

5. Transfer to serving bowls and top each bowl with a scoop of cooked rice, sliced green onions, and fresh parsley.

gulf coast oyster mushroom SOUP

Serves 4–6 (makes about 2 quarts) **GF**

When I first started working on this recipe, I thought, "This is going to be awful, but I'm gonna play around with it and see what happens." And whoops! I loved it. This soup has such a "Nola" feel, and the hearts of palm and oyster mushrooms mimic seafood in the best "so close it's kinda creepy" way. Before you begin, make sure to pre-chop all your veggies! Otherwise, you may find yourself feeling stressed about the timing. If you've got access to fresh lion's mane mushrooms, I recommend throwing in about a cup of those, too. They're kinda weird, but I think all of the best things are.

STUFF YOU NEED

- 4 tablespoons vegetable oil, divided
- 1 (15-ounce) can hearts of palm, stalks chopped into ½-inch-thick rounds
- ¼ cup all-purpose flour (for gluten-free, use rice flour instead)
- 1½ cups chopped celery (about 3 medium stalks)
- 1 cup chopped yellow onion (about ½ medium onion)
- ¾ cup chopped yellow bell pepper (about ½ medium pepper)
- ¾ cup chopped orange bell pepper (about ½ medium pepper)
- 1½ teaspoons minced garlic
- 1½ cups roughly chopped oyster mushrooms
- 5 cups water
- 2½ Not-Chick'n bouillon cubes
- 1 (15-ounce) can diced tomatoes
- ½ (8×8-inch) sheet dried roasted nori seaweed paper, crumbled
- 2 teaspoons Krimsey's Cajun Seasoning (page 193)
- 1 teaspoon salt
- ⅛ teaspoon ground bay leaf (or 1 whole bay leaf)
- 1 tablespoon chopped fresh parsley

Recommended side: cooked rice

WHAT TO DO

1. Heat 2 tablespoons vegetable oil in a 3-quart (or larger) pot over medium heat.

2. When oil is hot, add hearts of palm and cook, stirring, for 6–7 minutes, or until palm begins to turn golden brown.

3. Add flour and mix well to coat palm. Throw in remaining 2 tablespoons vegetable oil and your celery, onion, yellow bell pepper, and orange bell pepper. Increase heat to medium-high and sauté for 3–4 minutes, or until veggies begin to soften slightly.

4. Add garlic and oyster mushrooms and cook for 4–5 more minutes, stirring about once per minute. This will give you some nice dark spots on the bottom of your veggies and palm. The palm should be breaking down by now and beginning to look a bit like shredded crab. Don't be afraid to let the stuff at the bottom of the pot blacken a bit...remember, you're making Cajun food!

5. Add water, bouillon cubes, diced tomatoes, nori, Cajun seasoning, salt, and ground bay leaf. Bring to a simmer, then cook for about 12 minutes, or until flavors are incorporated and all veggies are soft.

6. Remove from the heat and add chopped parsley. Serve with rice.

new orleans **POBOY**

This was the most popular item on the menu at my Cajun vegan restaurant in North Hollywood, California. The combination of savory palm, fresh local sourdough bread, and homemade Cajun Ranch really made it something special. When people would ask what it tasted like, my usual response was, "just trust me...you'll love it." And they always did.

STUFF YOU NEED

1   batch Hearts of Palm Nuggets (page 119)

4   (6-inch) French sourdough rolls

Toppings: vegan mayo, shredded lettuce, beefsteak tomatoes (sliced ⅓-inch thick), dill pickles, Cajun Ranch (page 181)

WHAT TO DO

1. Preheat the oven to 350°F.

2. Make sure you have all of your sandwich ingredients ready to go so that when your fried palm nuggets come out of the fryer oil, you're ready to toss them straight on the bun.

3. Just before you drop your nuggets into the fryer oil, cut open your sourdough rolls (if they haven't already been pre-cut) and toast them on the middle oven rack for 6–8 minutes, or until barely golden brown and toasty.

4. Spread vegan mayo over the bottom of each roll, then layer on shredded lettuce, sliced tomatoes, dill pickles, Hearts of Palm Nuggets, and Cajun Ranch.

5. Serve immediately while the bread is still warm and flaky!

swamp queen POBOY

Another favorite at my Cajun vegan restaurant in North Hollywood, this queen of a sandwich is ridiculous to make. It's quite a task to cook at home due to the number of ingredients required and the timing of all of the hot items, but I expect that many of you die-hards will still go for it! I love it. Just try to time your fried items so that they finish at about the same time.

A fun little fact for you…in 2020 I was prepping to open my second restaurant in the Silver Lake neighborhood of Los Angeles. It was going to be a small sister poboy shop called "Swamp Queen!" Unfortunately, COVID-19 hit and plans changed, but I've enjoyed the change of pace and scenery. Everything happens for a reason.

STUFF YOU NEED

1   batch Hearts of Palm Nuggets (page 119)

5   cups hot Cajun Jambalaya (page 109)

12–16 Cajun Potato Wedges (page 155)

4   (6-inch) French sourdough rolls

Toppings: vegan mayo, lettuce (your choice), beefsteak tomatoes (sliced ⅓-inch thick), dill pickles, sliced green onions, shredded red cabbage, Cajun Ranch (page 181)

WHAT TO DO

1. Preheat the oven to 350°F.

2. Make sure you have all of your sandwich ingredients ready to go so that when your palm nuggets and potato wedges come out of the fryer oil, you're ready to toss them straight on the bun. You'll also want your jambalaya to be hot and ready to go.

3. Just before you drop your nuggets and wedges into the fryer oil, cut open your sourdough rolls (if they haven't already been pre-cut) and toast on the middle oven rack for 6–8 minutes, or until barely golden brown and toasty.

4. Spread vegan mayo on the bottom of each roll, then layer on lettuce, hot jambalaya, tomatoes, dill pickles, Hearts of Palm Nuggets, Cajun Potato Wedges, green onions, red cabbage, and Cajun Ranch. (It's going to be messy…that's the fun part!)

5. Serve immediately, and maybe have a fork handy.

veggie sausage **POBOY**

Makes 4 poboys

If you aren't living in New Orleans, where the bread used for poboys is typically a little lighter and fluffier than traditional rolls, then you can use French sourdough rolls, Vietnamese banh mi sandwich rolls, or hoagie rolls. It's extremely important that you use bread that is light and airy with a thin, crispy outside. Tough bread will ruin the authenticity!

STUFF YOU NEED

4   (6-inch) French sourdough rolls

2   teaspoons olive oil

4   vegan sausage links (spicy flavor recommended), sliced open lengthwise

Toppings: vegan mayo, shredded lettuce (iceberg recommended), beefsteak tomatoes (sliced ⅓ inch thick), thinly sliced red onion, dill pickles, Creole mustard (or Dijon mustard), avocado slices, hot sauce

WHAT TO DO

1. Preheat your oven to 350°F.

2. Cut open your sourdough rolls (if they haven't already been pre-cut) and toast on the middle oven rack for 6–8 minutes, or until barely golden brown and toasty.

3. While bread is toasting, heat olive oil in a skillet over medium heat. Add vegan sausage and cook for about 2 minutes on each side, or until barely darkened.

4. Spread vegan mayo over the bottom of each roll, then layer on shredded lettuce, sliced tomatoes, red onion, dill pickles, hot vegan sausage, and Creole mustard.

5. Serve immediately while the bread is still warm and flaky. Top with hot sauce for a Southern kick, and avocado for some West Coast flair. Dig in.

fried green tomato POBOY

A natural extension of my very well-loved Fried Green Tomatoes recipe, this poboy is one of my favorites because of its flavor combinations (Rémoulade Sauce and Smoky Maple Bacon Bits were made for each other) and its gorgeous colors. I love eating rainbow foods. Red tomatoes seem to be everywhere, so they're often what people default to when they think of tomatoes. But to me, the firmer and more acidic green tomato is much more appealing. If you hate squishy foods, like I do, give green tomatoes a chance! They're different, I swear.

STUFF YOU NEED

1 batch Fried Green Tomatoes (page 135)

4 (6-inch) French sourdough rolls

Toppings: vegan mayo, shredded iceberg lettuce, shredded red cabbage, sliced green onions, Smoky Maple Bacon Bits (page 196), Rémoulade Sauce (page 185)

WHAT TO DO

1. Preheat your oven to 350°F.

2. Make sure you have all of your sandwich ingredients ready to go so that when your fried green tomatoes come out of the fryer oil, you're ready to toss them straight on the poboy roll.

3. Just before you drop your tomato slices into the fryer oil, cut open your sourdough rolls (if they haven't already been pre-cut) and toast on the middle oven rack for 6–8 minutes, or until barely golden brown and toasty.

4. Spread vegan mayo on the bottom of each roll, then layer on shredded lettuce, fried green tomatoes (about 3 per sandwich), shredded red cabbage, green onions, Smoky Maple Bacon Bits, and Rémoulade Sauce.

5. Serve immediately while the bread is still warm and flaky.

pride POBOY

We brought this poboy to my restaurant's menu in 2017 to celebrate our community. Ten percent of all proceeds were donated to a local organization benefiting LGBTQ+ youth, who are statistically at a higher risk than their peers for being targets of bullying and/or victims of suicide. I don't know if it was the vibrant colors and rich flavors that made this a hit, or if it was a community eager to step up to show support to its most at-risk members; I like to believe it was both.

STUFF YOU NEED

1   batch Hearts of Palm Nuggets (page 119)
4   (6-inch) French sourdough rolls

Toppings: vegan mayo, shredded iceberg lettuce, beefsteak tomatoes (sliced ⅓-inch thick), shredded carrots, banana peppers, spinach, shredded red cabbage, Cali-Cajun Sauce (page 179)

WHAT TO DO

1. Preheat your oven to 350°F.

2. Make sure you have all of your sandwich ingredients ready to go so that when your fried palm nuggets come out of the fryer oil, you're ready to toss them straight on the bun.

3. Just before you drop your nuggets into the fryer oil, cut open your sourdough rolls (if they haven't already been pre-cut) and toast on the middle oven rack for 6–8 minutes, or until barely golden brown and toasty.

4. Spread vegan mayo on the bottom of each roll, then layer on shredded lettuce, tomato slices, shredded carrots, fried palm, banana peppers, spinach, red cabbage, and Cali-Cajun Sauce to create a rainbow.

5. Serve immediately while the bread is still warm and flaky!

oyster mushroom **POBOY**

Makes 4 poboys

These meaty oyster mushrooms make the perfect poboy. Ironically, it was never served in my restaurant. I used to really despise all mushrooms, so there was no chance I was going to serve a poboy stuffed with them. However, for the past couple of years, I've been challenging myself to take one bite of mushrooms whenever I have the chance. This exposure therapy has (shockingly) actually worked! I still think most mushrooms are gross, but these oyster mushrooms are delicious (especially fried). Maybe next year I'll try one raisin per month and see what happens.

STUFF YOU NEED

1   batch Fried Oyster Mushrooms (page 131)
4   (6-inch) French sourdough rolls

Toppings: vegan mayo, shredded lettuce, beefsteak tomatoes (sliced ⅓-inch thick), dill pickles, chopped fresh parsley, Rémoulade Sauce (page 185), fresh lemon wedges

WHAT TO DO

1. Preheat the oven to 350°F.

2. Make sure you have all of your sandwich ingredients ready to go so that when your oyster mushrooms come out of the fryer oil, you're ready to toss them straight on the bun.

3. While the oven is preheating, prepare your fried oyster mushrooms.

4. Just before oyster mushrooms are finished, cut open your sourdough rolls (if they haven't already been pre-cut) and toast on the middle oven rack for 6–8 minutes, or until barely golden brown and toasty.

5. Spread vegan mayo over the bottom of each roll, then layer on shredded lettuce, sliced tomato, dill pickles, hot oyster mushrooms, fresh parsley, and Rémoulade Sauce. Serve with fresh lemon wedges.

Cajun Jambalaya

Entrees

This is a dish that is extremely unique to Louisiana and is the "pie cousin" to étouffée. It's creamy, a little spicy, and full of seafood-y flavor. If you're nervous about DIYing the pie crust, don't be—it's simple!

STUFF YOU NEED

- 1 (15-ounce) can whole hearts of palm, cut into ½-inch rounds
- ¼ cup plus 1 tablespoon vegan butter, divided
- ⅛ teaspoon paprika
- ¼ cup all-purpose flour
- ¾ cup diced yellow onion (about ½ small onion)
- ½ cup chopped celery, cut into ⅓-inch-thick crescents (about 2 stalks)
- ⅓ cup diced red bell pepper (about ½ small pepper)
- ⅓ cup diced green bell pepper (about ½ small pepper)
- ⅓ cup diced yellow bell pepper (about ½ small pepper)
- 2 teaspoons minced garlic
- 1 cup chopped white mushrooms
- 1 cup chopped oyster mushrooms
- 1½ cups water
- 1 Not-Chick'n bouillon cube
- 1 cup diced tomatoes
- 2 teaspoons apple cider vinegar
- 2 teaspoons Krimsey's Cajun Seasoning (page 193)
- ½ teaspoon unsulphured molasses

WHAT TO DO

1. Preheat the broiler to high.

2. Place hearts of palm in a small bowl and drizzle with 1 tablespoon of melted vegan butter. Transfer to a baking pan and broil on the middle rack for 8 minutes. Remove from the oven, sprinkle with paprika, and stir before returning to the oven for another 6 minutes. Set aside.

3. Before moving on to the next step, make sure all of your veggies, 'shrooms, and tomatoes are chopped and ready to go.

4. In a 4-quart pot over medium heat, heat the remaining ¼ cup vegan butter. When melted, add the flour and stir continuously with a flat-bottomed spoon, scraping the bottom as you go, to make your roux. The roux will look puffy at first but will smooth out in a few minutes. Keep stirring until roux is the color of light peanut butter, about 5 minutes, then toss in onion, celery, and bell peppers.

5. Cook veggies for 4 minutes, then add garlic and mushrooms (both kinds) and cook for 2 more minutes.

6. Add water, Not-Chick'n bouillon, tomatoes, apple cider vinegar, Cajun seasoning, molasses, nori, celery salt, mace, black pepper, cayenne pepper, and bay leaf. Simmer for 10–12 minutes, or until liquid thickens. Remove from the heat and add broiled palm and fresh parsley. Set aside.

7. Preheat the oven to 350°F and remove one of the dough balls from the fridge. Flour your surface and use a rolling pin to roll out a dough circle that's ⅛–¼ inch thick and 11–12 inches in diameter. Transfer it to a 9-inch pie dish and use your fingers to press it into shape. Trim off the excess edges.

(Ingredients continue on next page)

(Recipe continues on next page)

(Recipe & ingredients continued from previous page)

¼   (8×8-inch) sheet dried roasted
     nori seaweed paper, crumbled

¼   teaspoon celery salt

¼   teaspoon ground mace

¼   teaspoon freshly
     cracked black pepper

⅛   teaspoon cayenne pepper

⅛   teaspoon ground bay leaf
     (or 1 whole bay leaf)

1½ tablespoons chopped fresh parsley

2   pie crust dough balls (Maw Maw's
     Pie Crust, page 202)

8. Pour in your filling, then repeat the crust rolling process with the second dough ball. Carefully place top dough circle over bottom crust/filling, then use a fork to press the outer edges together. With a sharp knife, cut some vents into the top piece to let out steam.

9. Bake 60–75 minutes on a lower rack, or until the top crust begins to brown. If the edges are getting darker faster than the rest of the pie, cover them with foil to slow down the browning process.

10. Remove from the oven and allow to cool slightly before serving.

blackened cajun **TEMPEH**

These strips are packed with intense Cajun taste, and they melt like butter in your mouth. The crispy texture of the blackened spice layer adds a unique flair that will get you hooked. Try the same technique on other foods (like sliced cauliflower)!

STUFF YOU NEED

1   (8-ounce) package tempeh

1½   cups no-chicken broth (or low-sodium vegetable stock)

4   tablespoons olive oil, divided

3   tablespoons Krimsey's Cajun Seasoning (page 193)*

Dipping sauce: Bourbon Street Sauce (page 183)

Note: *If you're using a Cajun seasoning other than the one on page 193, make sure it's low-sodium. This recipe uses a lot of seasoning, and an overly salty variety can really overpower everything here.

WHAT TO DO

1. Slice tempeh into 4 even sections (working from one short side to the other). Then chop each section in half (thickness-wise) so that you wind up with 8 pieces total that are about ⅓-inch thick each.

2. In a saucepan large enough to fit all the tempeh strips without overlapping, heat broth over medium heat.

3. Add tempeh strips and reduce the heat to medium-low. Cook at a simmer until no liquid is left in the pan, 15–20 minutes.

4. Remove tempeh from the heat and place in a container with a lid. Add 2 tablespoons of oil to the container, then shake gently to coat tempeh strips.

5. Spread Cajun seasoning on a small plate, then roll tempeh strips around in it to coat thoroughly.

6. Clean out your saucepan. Add the remaining 2 tablespoons of oil to the clean pan and return to the stovetop over medium-high heat.

7. Once the oil is heated, add tempeh and cook for 45 seconds to 1 minute on each side, or until a crispy black coat of seasoning forms around the tempeh.

8. Serve with Bourbon Street Sauce. If you don't feel up to the challenge of messing with your own sauce, store-bought BBQ sauce, mustard, and ketchup also make great dips for this dish! Have leftovers? Use them on top of a big Cajun Caesar Salad (page 64)!

deep south pasta CASSEROLE

For this recipe, no pasta pre-cooking is required—just throw everything into the casserole dish! I don't like doing extra dishes, so I love a recipe that keeps things simple. This colorful casserole is full of all the most comforting foods, so don't feel ashamed if you decide to skip plates...go ahead, just eat it straight out of the pan like a family of raccoons digging in fresh trash.

STUFF YOU NEED

- 1   (12-ounce) box tricolor rotini pasta
- 4   cups water
- 2   cups unsweetened non-dairy milk (rice milk recommended)
- 1   (14.5-ounce) can diced fire-roasted tomatoes, with juice
- 1   (6-ounce) can tomato paste
- 1½ cups frozen vegan beef crumbles
- ½   cup diced yellow onion (about ½ small onion)
- ½   cup diced red bell pepper (about ½ small pepper)
- ½   cup diced orange bell pepper (about ½ small pepper)
- ½   cup diced yellow bell pepper (about ½ small pepper)
- 3   teaspoons hot sauce
- 1¼ teaspoons salt
- 1   teaspoon minced garlic
- ½   teaspoon freshly cracked black pepper
- ½   teaspoon white pepper
- ½   teaspoon garlic powder
- ¼   teaspoon liquid smoke
- 2   cups vegan cheddar cheese shreds, divided
- ⅔   cup breadcrumbs

WHAT TO DO

1. Preheat your oven to 375°F.

2. Grease the bottom of a 9×13-inch casserole dish, then toss in the dry pasta. Add all remaining ingredients except 1 cup of the cheese and the breadcrumbs (you'll need those for topping). Mix and cover with foil. (Note: The pasta mixture will nearly reach the top of the dish; you'll need to stir it carefully to avoid spilling. If you are prone to messes, you can mix dry pasta and remaining ingredients (except 1 cup of cheese and breadcrumbs) in a large mixing bowl first, and then transfer to baking dish. You'll dirty an extra bowl, but maybe save yourself from mopping tomato juices off the floor.

3. Carefully transfer to the oven and bake for 40 minutes.

4. Remove from the oven, top with the remaining 1 cup of cheese and bread-crumbs, then bake, uncovered, for another 20 minutes. If you want an extra-browned top, set your oven to broil and crisp it up for a few extra minutes.

5. Let cool 5–10 minutes before serving, then dig in!

cajun red pepper ALFREDO

Serves 2–4 **GF**

This recipe was inspired by Cajun Chicken Alfredo, which I ordered without question at every restaurant that offered it until I hit my twenties. When I switched to a plant-based diet, I still craved that creamy pasta taste, so I made my own. This variation on my original alfredo recipe feels even more special, because you can only have it if you make it yourself.

STUFF YOU NEED

2   teaspoons olive oil

1   cup diced red bell pepper
     (about 1 small pepper)

2   tablespoons minced garlic, divided

1   (12-ounce) block silken tofu*

½   cup no-chicken broth
     (or vegetable stock)

5   tablespoons vegan butter,
     melted and divided

2   tablespoons vegan parmesan
     cheese crumbles

1   tablespoon nutritional yeast

1   tablespoon Krimsey's Cajun
     Seasoning (page 193)

2   teaspoons fresh lemon juice

½   teaspoon onion powder

¼   teaspoon salt, or to taste

1   (13-ounce) package dry tagliatelle
     pasta or fettuccine (make sure pasta
     is egg-free; can also use gluten-free,
     if desired)

8   ounces baby mixed mushrooms,
     chopped (about 3 cups)

Toppings: fresh chopped parsley, freshly cracked black pepper, and vegan parmesan cheese crumbles

Note: *Silken tofu is usually found in the Asian food section, not with the refrigerated tofu. It's very different from "regular" (firm) tofu, and has a totally different flavor and texture. So no subbing here!

WHAT TO DO

1. Heat oil in a small saucepan over medium heat. Add red bell peppers and sauté for 4–5 minutes, until they begin to soften. Add 1 tablespoon of the garlic and cook 1–2 more minutes, or until garlic is fragrant and light brown. Set aside to cool.

2. To make your sauce, combine silken tofu, broth, 4 tablespoons of the vegan butter, vegan parmesan cheese crumbles, nutritional yeast, Cajun seasoning, lemon juice, onion powder, and salt in a food processor and puree just enough to blend the flavors. When red peppers have cooled enough to handle, add those to the food processor and blend for 2 minutes. Scrape the sides and blend for 2 more minutes. Set aside.

3. In a 4-quart or larger pot, cook pasta in salted water according to package instructions, then drain and return to the pot. If needed, add a small drizzle of olive oil to your pasta after draining to keep it from getting sticky.

4. While pasta is cooking, melt the remaining 1 tablespoon butter in a large saucepan over medium heat. Add remaining 1 tablespoon of garlic and the chopped mushrooms. Sauté for 4–5 minutes, or until mushrooms begin to soften. Then, turn the heat to medium-high and cook for about 10 more minutes, or until 'shrooms turn medium-golden brown with some dark edges.

5. When ready to serve, add sauce to the pot of pasta. It's important to wait until the exact moment you're ready to serve, because the pasta will begin soaking up the sauce the second you add it to the pot.

6. If pasta and sauce have cooled, place over low heat just until hot, then add cooked mushrooms.

7. Top with fresh parsley, black pepper, and vegan parmesan cheese crumbles. Serve immediately.

bbq tofu FILLETS

If you're anything like me, you've struggled with how to make tofu that isn't a flavorless, watery blob. I've spent countless hours pressing, dabbing, and squeezing blocks of tofu to try and make it work. Now, I just do this! It takes a little time in the oven to dry out the water, but it's still much easier than my old methods. Enjoy! This super tasty BBQ tofu dish pairs well with Yukon and Russet Mash (page 161) and Cranberry Pecan Coleslaw (page 151).

STUFF YOU NEED

1   (14–16-ounce) block extra-firm tofu

½   cup Sweet Chili BBQ Sauce (page 173), or store-bought BBQ sauce

1   tablespoon vegetable oil

2   teaspoons minced garlic

½   small red onion, slivered (about ½ cup)

Topping: fresh cilantro

WHAT TO DO

1. Preheat the oven to 375°F.

2. Cut tofu block into ½-inch-thick strips (you should get about 8 fillets) and spread out on an oiled baking sheet. Bake for 30 minutes, or until edges start to brown slightly.

3. Meanwhile, mix BBQ sauce, vegetable oil, and garlic in a small bowl. Set aside.

4. After about 30 minutes, remove tofu from the oven and use tongs to dip the hot strips into the BBQ mixture, turning to coat. If the baking sheet is dry, re-oil it, then return tofu strips to the baking sheet. When all fillets have been coated front and back, you should have some sauce left over. Transfer red onion slivers to the bowl and mix to coat in the leftover sauce. Top tofu fillets on the pan with the red onions.

5. Bake for another 20–25 minutes, or until red onions begin to reduce, the sauce darkens a tad, and the edges of your tofu blacken. If any of your onions or sauce ooze over and get completely scorched, just trim them off with a sharp knife.

6. Remove from the oven, top with fresh cilantro, and serve.

peppery TOFU

Serves 2 **GF**

This one is spicy, but I wouldn't call it "fire alarm" spicy. So keep adding Tabasco sauce until it suits you. It pairs well with the One-Pot Mardi Gras Medley (page 138) and Black Sheep Slaw (page 152) to make a full meal.

STUFF YOU NEED

- 1 (14–16-ounce) block extra-firm tofu
- 1 tablespoon Tabasco sauce
- 1 tablespoon vegetable oil or olive oil
- 1 tablespoon balsamic vinaigrette
- ½ teaspoon freshly cracked black pepper
- ½ teaspoon Krimsey's Cajun Seasoning (page 193)
- ¼ teaspoon liquid smoke
- ¼ teaspoon salt
- 2 tablespoons sliced green onions

WHAT TO DO

1. Preheat the oven to 375°F.

2. Cut tofu block crosswise into ½-inch-thick strips (you should get about 8 strips). Spread tofu strips out on an oiled baking sheet. No need to press or towel off!

3. Bake for 30 minutes, flipping strips over at the 15-minute mark.

4. Meanwhile, mix Tabasco sauce, oil, balsamic vinaigrette, black pepper, Cajun seasoning, liquid smoke, and salt in a small bowl. Set aside.

5. Remove tofu from the oven and let strips cool for a few minutes so that you're able to handle them.

6. Dip each tofu strip into the hot sauce mixture, turning to coat. Return strips to the baking sheet and pour any leftover hot sauce mixture over the top. Sprinkle with sliced green onions.

7. Bake for 15 more minutes, or until edges are crispy.

8. Serve hot. Add more hot sauce for an extra kick.

beet & sweet potato CHILI

Beets add a sweet note to this chili recipe and give a beautiful, "murdery" color to the dish. Warning: don't let kids eat this indoors without strict supervision. Your house may wind up looking like a crime scene.

STUFF YOU NEED

- 2 tablespoons olive oil, plus extra as needed
- 2 medium beets, peeled and chopped into ½-inch pieces
- 1 medium orange sweet potato, chopped into ½-inch pieces, skin on
- 1 large crown broccoli, chopped
- 1 small white onion, chopped
- ½ bunch kale
- 1 (15-ounce) can diced fire-roasted tomatoes, with juice
- 1 (15-ounce) can kidney beans, drained
- 1 (15-ounce) can chickpeas, drained
- 1 (4-ounce) can fire-roasted and diced green chiles
- 2 cups low-sodium vegetable stock
- 1½ teaspoons chili powder
- ½ teaspoon garlic powder
- ½ teaspoon cumin
- ½ teaspoon salt, or to taste
- ¼ teaspoon red pepper flakes

Recommended toppings: potato chips or saltine crackers

WHAT TO DO

1. Warm oil in a large pot over medium heat. Throw in beets and cook for 4–6 minutes, stirring occasionally.

2. Add sweet potatoes and sauté for another 10–15 minutes, or until beets and sweet potatoes can be fairly easily pierced with a fork (but don't over-cook them; you still have to add some other veggies, too!). If things get sticky, add another tablespoon of oil.

3. Toss in the broccoli and onion and cook for another 5 minutes, or until broccoli is bright green.

4. Tear kale into pieces with your hands and add to the pot, then add all remaining ingredients. Simmer uncovered over medium heat until liquid is mostly gone, about 15 minutes, then reduce the heat to medium-low and simmer for another 10 minutes to allow flavors to combine.

5. Allow to cool slightly, then top with potato chips or saltines, if desired, and serve!

Krimfession Time...

Putting potato chips on top of food might be frowned upon in some places, but I don't really care about those places.

butternut squash GOULASH

Goulash actually has its roots in Hungary, but for me, this variation conjures up feelings of Southern warmth and hospitality. It was a dish that I commonly made for myself after first going vegan at age twenty in Louisiana, when I couldn't figure out what the heck I was supposed to be eating. It's filling, tasty, and homey, and made mostly from things that can be stocked in the pantry and freezer for when you need a quick meal. You can even stock some frozen butternut squash cubes in your freezer if you don't feel like chopping a single thing.

STUFF YOU NEED

2   teaspoons olive oil

2½ cups chopped butternut squash (½-inch cubes, seeds and skin removed; about ½ medium squash)

½   cup diced white onion

2   teaspoons minced garlic

½   (16-ounce) package elbow macaroni* (about 2 cups dry; can also use gluten-free pasta)

1   (24-ounce) jar traditional red pasta sauce

2   cups frozen vegan beef crumbles (can also use gluten-free version)

1   (15-ounce) can diced tomatoes, with juice

1   (15-ounce) can kidney beans, drained

1   cup corn kernels, fresh or frozen

2   teaspoons Krimsey's Cajun Seasoning (page 193)

½   teaspoon freshly cracked black pepper

¼   teaspoon salt, or to taste

2   big handfuls spinach (about 1 cup tightly packed)

Topping: fresh parsley

Note: *You can use the full box if you want, but it will create a drier, more noodely dish.

WHAT TO DO

1. Heat oil in a large, deep saucepan over medium heat. Add squash and cook, stirring every couple of minutes, for about 15 minutes, or until mostly tender. Add onions and garlic and cook for another 5–7 minutes, stirring occasionally, until squash can be easily pierced with a fork and onions are tender. Set aside.

2. While squash is cooking, bring a 4-quart pot of salted water to a boil and cook elbow macaroni according to package instructions. When done cooking, drain water and return pasta to the pot.

3. Once squash is tender, add pasta sauce, vegan beef crumbles, diced tomatoes, kidney beans, corn, Cajun seasoning, black pepper, and salt to the saucepan. Lower heat to medium-low and stir until beef crumbles are hot. Add spinach and cook until just barely wilted, about 2–3 minutes.

4. Pour sauce mixture over pasta and serve immediately. Garnish with fresh parsley.

west coast PISTOLETTES

This dish is my personal adaption of Cajun pistolettes, which are stuffed and fried bread rolls traditionally served in the Lafayette area. If you live in the South, you may be able to get your hands on some authentic pistolette rolls. Otherwise, any bread roll will do—Kaiser rolls, dinner rolls, and hard rolls all work great. When I eat these, I kinda feel like I'm eating a savory dinner doughnut.

STUFF YOU NEED

- 2 teaspoons vegetable oil
- 2 cups chopped broccoli florets (about 1 regular head)
- ¾ cup diced white onion (about ½ small onion)
- 2½ teaspoons minced garlic, divided
- 1 cup unsweetened non-dairy milk
- 1½ cups vegan cheddar cheese shreds, divided
- 1 cup frozen vegan beef crumbles
- 1 teaspoon Tabasco sauce
- 1 teaspoon Krimsey's Cajun Seasoning (page 193)
- ¼ teaspoon salt
- ¼ teaspoon freshly cracked black pepper
- 4 large dinner bread rolls (I use vegan hard rolls)
- 1 teaspoon vegan butter, for brushing rolls

WHAT TO DO

1. Heat oil in a 4-quart pot over medium heat. Add broccoli and onion and sauté for 3–4 minutes, until onions begin to soften. Add 2 teaspoons of minced garlic and cook for 1–2 more minutes, stirring occasionally, until the broccoli is nearly tender and onion begins to brown in some places.

2. Mix in non-dairy milk, 1 cup of vegan cheese, vegan beef crumbles, Tabasco sauce, Cajun seasoning, salt, and black pepper.

3. Reduce the heat to medium-low and simmer for 3–5 minutes, or until most liquids have been cooked down and the mixture is thick and creamy. Remove from the heat and set aside.

4. While the mixture is cooking, preheat the oven to 350°F.

5. Use your fingers to create a small hole on the side of each bread roll. Pull out the insides of the bread rolls and set them aside.

6. Once cheesy broccoli mixture has cooled down enough to handle, add the remaining ½ cup vegan cheese and mix. Use a spoon to fill each hollowed-out bread roll with the filling. Use the removed insides of bread to plug the holes, then transfer stuffed rolls to a baking sheet.

7. Mix melted vegan butter and add remaining ½ teaspoon of garlic, then brush the tops of the rolls with garlic butter. Bake for 10–12 minutes, or until the tops are golden brown and flaky and the garlic is toasted.

8. Let cool slightly and serve.

mini festival **CORN DOGS**

Makes about 18 mini dogs (depending on the size of sausages used)

These corn dogs are absolutely delicious, and you get to eat them off a cute little stick! These are a huge hit at all gatherings. I recommend serving them with homemade Hunny Mustard.

STUFF YOU NEED

Oil for frying (canola recommended)

¾ cup cornmeal

¾ cup all-purpose flour

2½ teaspoons cane sugar

1½ teaspoons salt

⅛ teaspoon cayenne pepper

¾ cup plus 2 tablespoons unsweetened non-dairy milk (rice milk recommended)

2 tablespoons vegetable oil

2 tablespoons yellow mustard

6–8 links vegan sausage, each link cut crosswise into three pieces

Dipping sauce: Hunny Mustard (page 192)

Optional: shredded iceberg lettuce and shredded red cabbage, for plating

WHAT TO DO

1. If using a mini electric fryer, fill the fryer with oil and set the temperature to 375°F. To fry on the stovetop, review the important notes for success on page 21. For this recipe, you'll want to have at least 2 inches of oil in your frying pot. While the oil is heating, mix up your batter.

2. In a medium bowl, whisk together cornmeal, flour, sugar, salt, and cayenne pepper. Use a spatula to blend in non-dairy milk, vegetable oil, and mustard.

3. Once oil is at the right temperature, poke a toothpick into the end of one of the sausage pieces. Use the toothpick as a handle to roll the mini dog in the batter, coating it fully top to bottom. Use your spatula to help cover it, if needed. Pull the mini dog out of the batter and let a bit of the excess fall off, then flip the dog upright and let the batter ooze downward a bit before carefully dropping it in the oil. I recommend that you use tongs for this step, even though it's tempting to drop it into the oil by the toothpick.

4. Fry for 2½–3½ minutes, or until the batter is fluffy and golden brown.

5. Remove from oil and place on a paper towel-lined plate to absorb the extra oil.

6. After taste testing, continue to batter and fry your remaining dogs in small batches, 3–4 at a time. Serve fresh with Hunny Mustard for maximum enjoyment. If you want to beautify your dish, serve atop a small bed of shredded lettuce and red cabbage for some pops of color.

sloppy JOELLES

This is a healthier alternative to the "Manwich" version of Sloppy Joes I enjoyed as a kid. Also, this version doesn't require that you subject yourself to outdated, gendered food marketing! Enjoy the powerful feminine energy you will feel while getting these hearty, sloppy sandwiches all over the place.

STUFF YOU NEED

1   teaspoon olive oil

½   cup diced celery

½   cup diced white onion

2   teaspoons minced garlic

⅓   cup water

1   (6-ounce) can tomato paste

1   cup ketchup

2   tablespoons yellow mustard

1   teaspoon onion powder

½   teaspoon salt

½   teaspoon chili powder

2   cups frozen vegan beef crumbles
    (can also use gluten-free version)

1½ cups cooked kidney beans
    (or one 15-ounce can)

4   sesame hamburger buns
    (or gluten-free buns)

Recommended toppings: red onion, dill pickles, tomatoes, lettuce, mustard, vegan mayo

WHAT TO DO

1. Heat olive oil in a 2-quart pot over medium heat. Add celery and onion and cook for 3 minutes, stirring occasionally. Throw in garlic and cook for 1 more minute.

2. Reduce heat to medium-low and add water, tomato paste, ketchup, mustard, onion powder, salt, and chili powder. Bring up to a gentle simmer, then add vegan beef crumbles and kidney beans. Cook for another 5 minutes, stirring occasionally, until crumbles are heated through and flavors are incorporated.

3. Toast your buns, then scoop filling onto bottom half of each bun. Top Sloppy Joelles with your desired fixins'. Serve immediately and make a mess!

cajun **JAMBALAYA**

This jambalaya recipe was the one that put my NoHo restaurant on the map. It took me over sixty iterations to get it just right (yes, that's right...Six. Zero.). A little jambalaya history for you: Jambalaya most likely came about in Louisiana through the influence of either West African jollof rice or Spanish dish paella—probably both. Generally, Creole-style New Orleans cooking includes tomatoes, while more Cajun-style cooking does not. This is also the case with jambalaya—Cajun versions like this one typically don't include tomatoes, but Creole jambalayas do. Be sure to use vegetable oil with this recipe because the flavor of olive oil won't work as well. Also, don't try to substitute white rice for the parboiled rice listed below. It will be disastrous.

STUFF YOU NEED

- 1 tablespoon plus 2 teaspoons vegetable oil, divided
- ¾ cup chopped yellow onion (about ½ small onion)
- ¾ cup chopped red bell pepper (about ½ medium pepper)
- ¾ cup chopped green bell pepper (about ½ medium pepper)
- ¾ cup chopped celery (about 2 medium stalks)
- 1 tablespoon minced garlic (about 3 medium cloves)
- 3 cups water
- 1½ cups dry parboiled rice
- 2½ tablespoons Krimsey's Cajun Seasoning (page 193)
- ½ teaspoon salt
- ⅛ teaspoon ground bay leaf (or 1 whole bay leaf)
- 2–3 links spicy vegan sausage, sliced into ⅓-inch-thick half-moon shapes
- 1 cup shredded vegan chicken and/or vegan shrimp, optional
- 1½ cups cooked kidney beans (or one 15-ounce can)
- 1½ cups cooked black-eyed peas (or one 15-ounce can)

Toppings: diced red cabbage, sliced green onions, and Cali-Cajun Sauce (page 179)

WHAT TO DO

1. Heat 1 tablespoon of the vegetable oil in a 3-quart or larger pot over medium heat, then add onion, red bell pepper, green bell pepper, and celery. Sauté for 5 minutes, then add garlic and sauté another 1–2 minutes, or until onions are slightly translucent and garlic is fragrant.

2. Add water, parboiled rice, Cajun seasoning, salt, and bay leaf. Bring to a boil, then lower the heat to medium-low and cover. Simmer lightly for about 15 minutes, or until rice is cooked through. Stir every minute or so during the last 5 minutes of cooking, scraping the bottom of the pot as you go. If all your water absorbs and the rice is still crunchy, add more water, ¼ cup at a time, and simmer on low heat until absorbed.

3. While rice is cooking, heat remaining 2 teaspoons of vegetable oil in a medium saucepan over medium heat. Add vegan sausage slices and vegan chicken or shrimp, if using, and sauté for 6–8 minutes, or until slightly browned.

4. When rice is done cooking, remove from the heat and add kidney beans, black-eyed peas, vegan sausage, and vegan chicken/shrimp, if using. Stir, cover, and set aside off the heat to steam for an additional 10 minutes.

5. When ready to serve, if needed, reheat the jambalaya over low heat for 4–5 minutes until piping hot.

6. Portion into bowls and serve topped with diced red cabbage, sliced green onions, and Cali-Cajun Sauce.

"biscuits for dinner" CASSEROLE

My mom loved making chicken pot pies for us when we were kids—probably because I was such a weirdo for them. I swear I could eat a whole pie myself. I'd sneak back into the kitchen after dinner and keep picking at the crust like a rodent nibbling on floor crumbs in the dark. This is my biscuit-loving tribute to my mother's chicken pot pies, complete with the frozen bagged veggies that will never go out of style.

STUFF YOU NEED

Biscuit Topping

- 3 cups all-purpose flour
- 1 tablespoon baking powder
- 1 teaspoon salt
- ¼ cup plus 2 tablespoons chilled vegan butter, plus extra for brushing
- 1 cup unsweetened non-dairy milk, chilled (rice milk recommended)

Filling

- 2 cups unsweetened non-dairy milk
- 1½ cups low-sodium vegetable stock
- 3 tablespoons Bragg liquid aminos, or soy sauce
- 3 tablespoons all-purpose flour
- 2 tablespoons nutritional yeast
- 1 teaspoon dried thyme
- 1 teaspoon salt
- ½ teaspoon onion powder
- ½ teaspoon garlic powder
- ½ teaspoon dried ground sage
- ½ teaspoon freshly cracked black pepper

WHAT TO DO

1. In a large bowl, whisk together flour, baking powder, and salt. Use a fork to cut in vegan butter, mashing it against the side of the bowl. Keep cutting it in until the dough looks kind of "gravelly" and there are no large butter chunks remaining.

2. Pour in non-dairy milk and stir until it gets too thick and you need to use your hands. Knead gently until the dough is just mixed—avoid over-kneading as it can make your biscuits tough. If your dough is sticky, sprinkle in a bit more flour until it feels like soft Play-Doh.

3. Cover the dough bowl and move it to the fridge to rest.

4. Preheat your oven to 350°F.

5. In a medium bowl, whisk together non-dairy milk, vegetable stock, liquid aminos, flour, nutritional yeast, thyme, salt, onion powder, garlic powder, sage, and black pepper for your filling.

6. Heat 2 tablespoons of the olive oil in a large, deep skillet over medium heat. Add tofu cubes and cook, stirring periodically for 5–7 minutes, until some sides are starting to turn light golden brown. Careful to keep your heat on medium—any higher and you could cause the oil to start spitting!

7. Add chopped potatoes, onion, and remaining oil and cook for another 6–8 minutes, stirring occasionally. Potatoes should be slightly undercooked, and tofu cubes should be golden brown.

(Ingredients continue on next page)

(Recipe continues on next page)

(Recipe & ingredients continued from previous page)

5   tablespoons olive oil, divided

8   ounces extra-firm tofu (about half a
    block), cut into ½-inch cubes

1   medium russet potato (about ½
    pound) cut into ½-inch cubes (about
    2 cups chopped)

½   cup diced yellow onion

1   cup sliced white mushrooms, ¼ inch
    thick

2   teaspoons minced garlic

1   (12-ounce) bag frozen mixed
    vegetables (corn, peas, carrots,
    green beans)

6   cups frozen hash browns
    (about 1 pound)

8. Add mushrooms, garlic, and mixed veggies, and continue cooking. After 2 minutes, add milk mixture and simmer on medium heat, scraping the bottom periodically, for 12–15 minutes, or until the sauce thickens up and the mushrooms are soft. Remove from the heat and set aside.

9. Lightly oil the bottom of a 9×13-inch casserole dish, then spread frozen hash browns evenly in the bottom of the dish.

10. Pour your hot filling on top of the hash browns and set the casserole dish aside.

11. Remove biscuit topping from the fridge. On a lightly floured work surface, roll out into 12×15-inch sheet ⅛–¼ inch thick. Lightly flour your rolling pin if the dough gets sticky. Use a cup or biscuit cutter to cut out biscuit shapes, then press a fork into the tops a few times to flatten and stylize. You should have about 20 rounds by the time you're done. More is okay!

12. Use dough rounds to cover your casserole filling. They can overlap slightly—no worries.

13. Brush the tops of biscuits with melted butter, then transfer the casserole dish to the oven. Bake for about 1 hour, or until biscuit tops turn golden brown.

14. Allow to cool slightly before cutting and serving.

heart of the bayou ÉTOUFFÉE

Serves 4–6 **GF**

Pronounced "ay-too-fay," this dish was inspired by the French word étouffer (which means "to smother"). It is believed that it was first served around the year 1920 in the backcountry bayous of Louisiana. It was originally a popular dish among Cajuns of the backwaters (made with crawfish), but it eventually made its way into many New Orleans restaurants as people tasted it and loved it.

STUFF YOU NEED

2 cups dry parboiled rice

¼ cup vegan butter

½ cup all-purpose flour (for gluten-free, use ¼ cup rice flour instead)

1 (14.5-ounce) can diced tomatoes, with juice

4 cups coarsely chopped onions (about 2 large onions)

2 cups coarsely chopped green bell pepper (about 1 large pepper)

2 cups coarsely chopped red bell pepper (about 1 large pepper)

2 cups coarsely chopped celery (about 4 stalks)

4 garlic cloves, minced

2 cups low-sodium vegetable stock, plus extra as needed

1 (15-ounce) can whole hearts of palm, crushed with hands

2 tablespoons Krimsey's Cajun Seasoning (page 193)

2 teaspoons salt

1 (8×8-inch) sheet dried roasted nori seaweed paper

½ teaspoon cayenne pepper

1 bay leaf

¼ cup chopped fresh parsley leaves

Recommended toppings: sliced green onions sliced green onions and battered vegan shrimp

WHAT TO DO

1. Cook rice according to package instructions and set aside.

2. While rice is cooking, melt vegan butter in a 4-quart pot over low heat.

3. Raise the heat to medium and add flour to make your roux. Stir continuously with a flat-bottomed spoon, scraping the bottom of the pan as you go, until the mixture is the color of peanut butter. This should take 4–6 minutes. I advise that you don't try to multitask while the roux is roasting, because you'll likely burn it! (At least, that's what usually happens to me...)

4. Add diced tomatoes and their juice, onions, bell peppers, celery, garlic, and ½ cup of the vegetable stock. Reduce the heat to medium-low and lightly simmer, stirring occasionally, until onions are translucent, about 10 minutes.

5. Add remaining 1½ cups stock, hearts of palm, Cajun seasoning, salt, crumbled nori paper, cayenne pepper, and bay leaf. Continue to simmer gently for another 20 minutes, or until the mixture is the consistency of a thick soup. If it's too thick for your liking, just add a little more stock until it's perfect.

6. Add fresh parsley, stir, and serve over rice. Top with green onions and battered vegan shrimp, if desired.

creamy red beans & parsley RICE

These beans always take me right back home, especially if I've got some crumbly cornbread and vegan butter to go with them. Red beans and rice was a commonly eaten dish growing up, and it was always consistent. It took me a long time to get this recipe right, because the red beans I grew up on set the bar so high.

You can make these in a slow cooker, too! Just toss all the ingredients (except the rice and fresh parsley) into the slow cooker and cook on high for 3–4 hours, or on low for 8–10 hours. Reduce the amount of liquid listed below to 1¾ cups water and 2 cups broth, since the slow cooker won't steam off as much liquid as the stovetop. All other ingredients stay the same. Using a slow cooker will take longer, but you won't have to watch it as closely as you would if you were cooking on the stovetop. It's a similar product with less work, so I get why one might opt for this route. If you want a creamier bean, though, go with the stovetop method.

STUFF YOU NEED

- 1 tablespoon olive oil
- 1 cup chopped yellow onion
- 1 cup chopped green bell pepper
- 1 cup chopped celery
- 5 teaspoons minced garlic
- 3 cups water
- 3 cups no-chicken broth (or low-sodium vegetable stock)
- 1 pound dried light red beans (2¼ cups), soaked and excess water drained off (see page 23 for soaking instructions)
- 1 tablespoon dried parsley
- 2 teaspoons Krimsey's Cajun Seasoning (page 193)
- 2 teaspoons salt, or to taste
- 2 teaspoons brown sugar
- 1 teaspoon liquid smoke
- 1 teaspoon dried thyme

WHAT TO DO

1. Heat olive oil in an 8-quart (or larger) pot over medium heat.

2. Add onion, bell pepper, celery, and garlic. Cook, stirring occasionally, for 4–5 minutes, or until veggies begin to soften.

3. Add water, broth, red beans, dried parsley, Cajun seasoning, salt, brown sugar, liquid smoke, thyme, sage, cayenne pepper, and bay leaf.

4. Reduce the heat to medium-low and simmer, uncovered, for 2½ hours, or until beans are tender and sauce is thick and creamy. The pot should be gently bubbling, but not foaming or aggressively boiling. Stir every 30 minutes to make sure nothing is sticking to the pot, and scrape the bottom of the pot with a flat-bottomed spoon every 5–10 minutes during the last half hour of cooking. If too much water is boiling off and things are getting sticky, add water 1 cup at a time to loosen up the beans. Note: If you're in a rush, you can turn up the heat and cook the beans faster. However, they won't have that same slow-cooked taste!

(Ingredients continue on next page)

(Recipe continues on next page)

(Recipe & ingredients continued from previous page)

½ teaspoon ground sage

¼ teaspoon cayenne pepper

⅛ teaspoon bay leaf powder
(or 1 whole bay leaf)

1 pound (or 2¼ cups) dry
parboiled rice

2 tablespoons chopped fresh parsley

Recommended toppings: pan-seared vegan sausage, sliced green onions, and hot sauce

5. When beans are about 30 minutes away from being done, cook rice according to package directions. Be sure to salt your rice water as directed on the package, because unsalted rice will dilute the flavors of your red beans when served together. If you're using bulk rice with no instructions, add 1 teaspoon of salt per pound of rice. When rice is finished, mix in fresh parsley and let sit for another 5 minutes.

6. When beans are finished cooking, use a large spoon to smash some of the beans up against the side of the pot to thicken the sauce. Smashing about ½ cup worth of beans should do the trick. Taste and add salt as desired.

7. Serve beans over cooked parsley rice and top with vegan sausage, sliced green onions, and/or hot sauce.

jambalaya collard **WRAPS**

Serves 1–2 (makes 2 medium wraps) **GF**

A super healthy wrap that makes use of leftover Cajun Jambalaya while incorporating some beautiful good-for-you greens.

STUFF YOU NEED

½ teaspoon salt

2 extra-large collard leaves

1 cup prepared Cajun Jambalaya (page 109), warmed

⅓ cup cooked corn kernels, warmed

⅓ cup shredded carrots

⅓ cup shredded red cabbage

Cajun Ranch (page 181)

WHAT TO DO

1. Fill a deep saucepan or wide pot—the wider, the better—with at least 1 inch of water, add the salt, and bring to a boil.

2. Prepare a large bowl of ice water and set aside.

3. Wash collards thoroughly, then slice out the thickest part of the stem, cutting into the leaf 2–3 inches toward the center.

4. Once water is boiling, cook collards by dunking them underwater for 30 seconds each. After 30 seconds, use tongs to remove them from the boiling water and dunk them in your bowl of ice water for 5–10 seconds to stop the cooking process and cool them down. This quick cook softens up the stems a bit for rolling, and makes the leaves more palatable.

5. Dry collards with a towel and lie them out flat, with the underside of the leaves facing upward, to prepare for assembly and rolling.

6. Scoop Cajun Jambalaya evenly on top of each leaf, keeping it centered toward the stem side of the leaf (where you just cut).

7. Layer warm corn, shredded carrots, and shredded red cabbage on top of the jambalaya, topping each wrap with Cajun Ranch as desired.

8. Wrap into a "burrito" by rolling up from the wide base of the leaf toward the narrow ("top") side. Stop halfway up the leaf, then fold the left and right sides inward toward the midline of the leaf. From there, continue rolling the wrap toward the skinny "top" of the leaf until you reach the tip.

9. Repeat with the second wrap.

10. If desired, use toothpicks to hold the wraps in place. For easiest eating and prettiest presentation, slice each wrap in half and serve with an extra side of Cajun Ranch.

hearts of palm NUGGETS

Serves 2–4 (makes 3–4 cups)

These nuggets are poppable and addictive, so if you're making them for the poboys on pages 77, 79, or 83, make sure you actually leave some for the sandwiches! As I was searching for a great vegan poboy filling idea, I just walked the aisles of stores, waiting for something to catch my eye. As soon as I saw the hearts of palm, I knew that was it before I even tasted it.

STUFF YOU NEED

Oil for frying (canola oil recommended)

½ cup all-purpose flour

3 tablespoons cornmeal

1 ½ tablespoons cornstarch

1 ¼ teaspoons salt

1 teaspoon baking powder

1 teaspoon freshly cracked black pepper

½ teaspoon paprika

½ teaspoon garlic powder

½ teaspoon onion powder

½ teaspoon chili powder

⅛ teaspoon cayenne pepper

1 cup unsweetened non-dairy milk (rice milk recommended)

1 (15-ounce) can hearts of palm

Dipping sauce: Ginger Cocktail Sauce (page 175)

WHAT TO DO

1. If using a mini electric fryer, fill the fryer with oil and set the temperature to 375°F. To fry on the stovetop, review the important notes for success on page 21. For this recipe, you'll want to have at least 1 inch of oil in your frying pot. While the oil is heating, mix up your batter.

2. In a large bowl, whisk together all dry ingredients, then use a spatula to mix in non-dairy milk. Save the hearts of palm for later.

3. If your palm is pre-chopped, skip this step. If you're working with whole hearts of palm, lie them out on a cutting board and slice them into ½-inch-thick bite-sized rounds. It's okay if they don't hold their shape perfectly.

4. Once your oil is at the correct temperature, use tongs to coat a palm piece in batter and then carefully place it in the frying oil. Cook for 2–3 minutes, or until the nugget is golden yellow-brown. Remove from oil and place on a paper towel-lined plate to absorb excess oil. Allow to cool before taste-testing.

5. If your nugget came out great, continue frying the rest of your batch. If not, adjust your heat up or down and give it another go. Nuggets should be fluffy and cooked through to the center.

6. For maximum tastiness, serve immediately with Ginger Cocktail Sauce.

Entrees 119

bayou goddess BOWL

I created this bowl for the restaurant after I began taking care of myself. I adopted a whole-food, plant-based diet, got sober, and dropped over thirty pounds. I found a new, healthier way of being. A goddess eats to nourish her body, and takes joy in consuming healthy, life-giving foods. On our very last day in business, we prepared this bowl for my favorite customer ever and the ultimate goddess: Lizzo. So now, I call it the "goddess bowl" for two reasons.

STUFF YOU NEED

1½ cups cooked rice, any kind

1 teaspoon olive oil

⅓ cup fresh corn kernels (or frozen works, too)

½ teaspoon minced garlic

⅔ cup low-sodium vegetable stock

⅓ cup cooked black-eyed peas

½ teaspoon Krimsey's Cajun Seasoning (page 193)

2 big handfuls shredded kale (2–3 ounces)

⅓ cup shredded carrots

⅓ cup diced red bell pepper

Toppings: Cajun Ranch (page 181), Krimsey's Cajun Seasoning, 2 tablespoons Smoky Maple Bacon Bits (page 196), 2 tablespoons diced red cabbage

WHAT TO DO

1. If you don't already have some cooked rice on hand, get that done first! This whole process is pretty quick, so I would recommend waiting to start until your rice is done.

2. Heat oil in a medium skillet or saucepan over medium heat. Add corn and garlic and sauté for 4 minutes, then add vegetable stock, black-eyed peas, and Cajun seasoning. Mix well, then add shredded kale. Use tongs to cover kale in liquids and spices, then cook for 2 minutes, or until kale is slightly wilted. Reduce heat to low to keep things warm.

3. Time to assemble the bowl! Put hot, cooked rice in your serving bowl. Line the edges with carrots and red bell pepper (leaving room in the center), then drizzle Cajun Ranch over rice and veggies.

4. Spoon your cooked kale-corn mixture over the rice, then top with a light sprinkle of Cajun seasoning, Smoky Maple Bacon Bits, and diced red cabbage.

5. Enjoy being a goddess.

bean & black-eyed pea CHILI

Serves 3–4 (makes about 8 cups)   **GF**

This was a New Year's special at the restaurant, and I've modified it here to be a quick-cook version. In the South, eating black-eyed peas on New Year's Day is thought to bring good luck and prosperity in the coming year. I'm not superstitious, but I like black-eyed peas, so I go along with it. Pair it with cornbread and collards for an extra-lucky New Year's Day meal, if you're into that. You can also use fire-roasted tomatoes if you like a little smoky, charred flavor.

STUFF YOU NEED

2   teaspoons olive oil

1½ cups peeled and sliced carrots, cut on the bias into ¼-inch discs (about 3 large carrots)

1   cup chopped white onion (about 1 medium onion)

¾   cup chopped green bell pepper (about ½ medium pepper)

¾   cup chopped red bell pepper (about ½ medium pepper)

1   teaspoon minced garlic

2   cups filtered water

1   (15-ounce) can diced tomatoes, with juice

1   (15-ounce) can black-eyed peas, drained

1   (15-ounce) can black beans, drained

1   (15-ounce) can kidney beans, drained

2   (4-ounce) cans diced green chiles

2   teaspoons salt

1   teaspoon chili powder

1   teaspoon garlic powder

1   teaspoon onion powder

1   teaspoon cumin

1   teaspoon freshly cracked black pepper

Topping suggestions: sliced green onions and crumbled saltine crackers or Fritos

WHAT TO DO

1. Heat oil in a 4-quart (or larger) pot over medium heat. Add carrots and cook, covered, stirring every couple minutes or so, for 5–7 minutes, or until carrots soften enough to be poked with a fork, but not easily.

2. Add onion and bell peppers, then cook another 3–4 minutes, or until veggies begin to soften. Add garlic and cook for another 2–3 minutes, until garlic is fragrant and just barely browned.

3. Add water, diced tomatoes, black-eyed peas, black beans, kidney beans, green chiles, salt, chili powder, garlic powder, onion powder, cumin, and black pepper. Bring to a boil, then cook, uncovered, for 10–15 minutes, or until water is mostly absorbed and all veggies are tender. If you prefer a more liquid chili (or if your water is boiling off too quickly), add water as desired, ½ cup at a time.

4. Portion into serving bowls and top with sliced green onions and crumbled saltines or Fritos. Or should I say *and* Fritos?

stuffed red BELL PEPPERS

I love food that is fun to look at, so stuffed peppers are a winner. For an even more colorful display, mix and match your bell pepper colors (yellow, red, and orange). In my opinion, you should stay away from green ones because they're a little more bitter. But if that's your thing, I'm not gonna yuck on your yum.

STUFF YOU NEED

1   teaspoon olive oil, plus extra for brushing bell peppers

½   cup diced yellow onion

2   teaspoons minced garlic

2¼ cups water

1   Not-Chick'n bouillon cube

1   cup dry parboiled rice

1   teaspoon dried thyme

½   teaspoon Krimsey's Cajun Seasoning (page 193)

½   teaspoon freshly cracked black pepper, plus extra for sprinkling peppers

¼   teaspoon salt, plus extra for sprinkling peppers

4   medium red bell peppers

1¼ cups frozen vegan beef crumbles (can also use gluten-free version)

⅔   cup corn kernels, fresh, frozen, or canned (about half a 15-ounce can)

⅔   cup cooked black beans (about half a 15-ounce can)

½   cup shredded vegan cheese blend (cheddar and mozzarella)

Toppings: vegan parmesan crumbles, fresh parsley, fresh thyme, and freshly cracked black pepper

WHAT TO DO

1. Preheat the oven to 400°F.

2. Heat oil in a 4-quart pot over medium heat. Add onion and cook for 2 minutes, then add garlic and cook, stirring often, for 1 more minute.

3. Increase heat to medium-high and add water. Once water starts boiling, add bouillon cube and stir well to dissolve. Once the cube is dissolved, reduce heat back down to medium and add rice, thyme, Cajun seasoning, black pepper, and salt. Cover and simmer gently for 10–15 minutes, or until liquids are absorbed and rice is tender. Scrape the bottom occasionally during the last 5 minutes of cooking to avoid sticking or burning. If it seems like the water is boiling off too quickly and your rice is dry, just add extra water ⅓ cup at a time.

5. Remove from the heat and set aside, covered, to steam for 10 minutes. Meanwhile, wash the red bell peppers and cut each one in half lengthwise, cutting through the stem to the bottom of the pepper. Scoop out seeds and membranes and discard, but leave the stems—they're pretty. If needed, shave a teeny tiny bit of flesh off the bottom side of each pepper half so they can sit on the pan without rocking around. Be careful not to cut through the peppers! But if you do, don't stress.

6. Brush the insides and cut edges of the peppers moderately with olive oil, then sprinkle with salt and pepper. Place cut sides down on a baking sheet and bake for 15 minutes.

7. Meanwhile, return to your pot of rice and add vegan beef crumbles, corn, and black beans. Stir well to distribute ingredients and set aside.

8. When the peppers are ready, flip to place cut side up on the pan. Distribute the rice stuffing evenly among the 8 pepper halves. Top with shredded vegan cheese and vegan parmesan crumbles, if desired. Bake for 20 minutes. If you have leftover stuffing, congratulations! You get to enjoy a snack. Serve immediately, topped with fresh parsley, fresh thyme, and freshly cracked black pepper.

cajun street TACOS

Makes 4 tacos **GF**

I created this special for a street food festival, Vegan Street Fair, in North Hollywood. It was the first big event I ever served at, and I continued to do it for years after because it was always such a massive success. With over 30,000 people in attendance, it was one of the largest crowds I'd ever served. Big kudos to Jess (the founder and event organizer) for making the whole thing happen every year!

STUFF YOU NEED

8   (4-inch) corn tortillas ("street taco" size)

Cali-Cajun Sauce (page 179) or Cajun Ranch (page 181) if you want something less spicy

1   cup prepared Cajun Jambalaya (page 109), heated

⅓   cup shredded lettuce

¼   cup diced red bell pepper

¼   cup finely shredded red cabbage

¼   cup sliced green onions

Toppings: fresh lemon or lime juice and freshly cracked black pepper

WHAT TO DO

1. Warm your tortillas. Heat a cast-iron skillet (a regular skillet is fine, too) over medium-high heat. Place 1–2 tortillas on the dry pan and cook 15–20 seconds on each side, or until brown spots start to form. You may also use a spatula or a small pot to press down on the tortillas for more even cooking. When finished, the tortillas should be browned in some places, but not crispy.

2. Stack two warmed tortillas together and drizzle some of your preferred sauce on the top one (each taco gets two tortillas). Add hot Cajun Jambalaya, shredded lettuce, red bell pepper, red cabbage, green onions, and another drizzle of sauce on top. Finish with a fresh lemon or lime squeeze and some freshly cracked black pepper.

3. Repeat for the rest of your tortillas and serve immediately.

chili jalapeño **BUTTERNUT SQUASH STEAKS**

Serves 4   GF

This one is for spice lovers only! If you like a little heat, but not fire, just omit the jalapeños and it will be tolerable. The base squash recipe is still kickin', but nothing like the full jalapeño-topped version. This is a great dish for people who eat food so spicy that it doesn't make sense to anyone else.

STUFF YOU NEED

1   medium butternut squash
     (about 2 pounds)
3   tablespoons vegetable oil
1½ teaspoons brown sugar
1½ teaspoons salt
1   teaspoon paprika
1   teaspoon chili powder
½   teaspoon garlic powder
½   teaspoon freshly cracked
     black pepper
¼   teaspoon cayenne pepper
2   jalapeños, 1 thinly sliced into rounds
     and 1 sliced into half-moons

Toppings: coarse-ground salt and freshly cracked black pepper

WHAT TO DO

1. Preheat the oven to 375°F.

2. Peel the squash using a vegetable peeler, making sure to remove the skin all the way to the orange/yellowish part (the white part is bitter).

3. Cut off the "neck" of the squash from the base, then cut the stem end off the neck. Set the base aside for now. Slice the neck lengthwise into 4 "steaks," each about ½ inch thick. This should give you 3–4 squash steaks. Trim the round edges from the two outer steaks to make them flatter, if desired.

4. Now, back to the base. Chop off a bit of the butt of the squash so it sits upright, then slice it in half from top to bottom. Use a spoon to remove the stringy stuff from the interior of the base, then slice it up into ½-inch-thick crescent shapes (it should look a lot like sliced cantaloupe).

5. Use a small, sharp knife to carve a shallow crosshatch pattern into both sides of the squash steak slabs and crescents. Set squash aside.

6. In a small, shallow bowl, mix together vegetable oil, brown sugar, salt, paprika, chili powder, garlic powder, black pepper, and cayenne pepper.

7. One by one, smoosh each squash piece into the spice rub. Use a spatula or your hands to cover all sides lightly, then transfer the squash to a parchment-lined (or lightly oiled) baking sheet. Top squash with jalapeño rounds and half-moons.

8. Bake for about 30 minutes, or until squash edges are dark brown and squash can be poked through with a fork.

9. Top with salt and pepper to taste and serve immediately.

One-Pot Mardi Gras Medley

Sides

fried oyster MUSHROOMS

I used to hate all non-psychedelic mushrooms, until I found oyster mushrooms. They are just so unique look-ing, and the flavor is a little milder to me compared to other varieties. They also resemble seafood (calamari, maybe?) in their taste and texture, which is interesting. And I love interesting.

STUFF YOU NEED

¾ cup unsweetened non-dairy milk (rice milk recommended)

1 tablespoon apple cider vinegar

½ pound oyster mushrooms, rinsed

Oil for frying (canola oil recommended)

½ cup all-purpose flour

3 tablespoons cornmeal

2½ tablespoons cornstarch

1 teaspoon salt

1 teaspoon freshly cracked black pepper

1 teaspoon garlic powder

1 teaspoon onion powder

½ teaspoon paprika

½ teaspoon chili powder

½ teaspoon cumin

⅛ teaspoon cayenne pepper

Toppings: vegan parmesan cheese crumbles and chopped fresh parsley

Dipping sauce: Rémoulade Sauce (page 185)

WHAT TO DO

1. In a small mixing bowl, combine non-dairy milk and apple cider vinegar.

2. Separate oyster mushrooms into chunks of whatever size you like. It's okay to leave several 'shrooms together on one branch—it's fun. Dump them into the bowl with the non-dairy milk-vinegar mixture, toss to coat, and let sit while you heat your frying oil.

3. If using a mini electric fryer, fill the fryer with oil and set the temperature to 375°F. To fry on the stovetop, review the important notes for success on page 21. For this recipe, you'll want to have at least 1 inch of oil in your frying pot.

4. In another small bowl, whisk together flour, cornmeal, cornstarch, salt, black pepper, garlic powder, onion powder, paprika, chili powder, cumin, and cayenne pepper. Set aside.

5. Once oil is at the right temperature, use tongs to remove a tester mush-room from the liquid and roll it in the flour mixture, smushing the batter into the gills and crevices.

6. Use your tongs to gently drop tester mushroom into the hot oil. Fry for 2 minutes, or until batter is golden brown. Remember that controlling frying temperatures on the stovetop can be tricky, so watch your 'shroomies and adjust the frying time as necessary.

7. When tester mushroom is finished cooking, use tongs to remove it and transfer to a paper towel-lined plate to cool for 1 minute. Sprinkle with vegan parmesan cheese and top with fresh parsley. Taste test it. All good? Continue with the rest of your shrooms. If it's under- or overdone, adjust the oil temperature as needed. Fry the rest in batches.

8. When the entire batch is finished, serve immediately with Rémoulade Sauce.

roasted accordion **POTATOES**

Adapted from Swedish Hasselback potatoes, this variation is spiced with traditional Cajun flavors. The shape of these reminds me of an accordion, a one-of-a-kind instrument and critical piece of a traditional zydeco band. Makes me miss live music nights with The High Life Cajun Band at the restaurant.

STUFF YOU NEED

4   medium russet potatoes
    (about 1 pound each)

⅓   cup vegan butter, melted

1   tablespoon Krimsey's Cajun
    Seasoning (page 193)

1   tablespoon minced garlic

Recommended toppings: Cajun Nacho Sauce (page 178) or Smoked Chili Cheeze Sauce (page 186), pickled jalapeños, and freshly cracked black pepper

WHAT TO DO

1. Preheat your oven to 400°F.

2. Wash and scrub your potatoes.

3. Use a sharp knife to cut thin slices into potatoes, a little over ¼-inch thick. Be careful not to cut all the way through the bottom of the potatoes—you want them to stay connected underneath so they hold together. I recommend using two chopsticks on either side of each potato to keep yourself from cutting all the way through. Just line up two chopsticks about 1 inch apart, then place your potato on top of them, with the center of the potato hitting the cutting surface. The chopsticks will work as a "guard" to keep you from cutting all the way through.

4. As you cut the potatoes, transfer them to a parchment-lined or lightly oiled baking sheet.

5. In a small bowl, stir together melted vegan butter, Cajun seasoning, and minced garlic. Brush butter mixture across tops of potatoes, sticking the brush down between slices to fully coat. You should have some left over—you don't need to use it all right now.

6. Bake for 30 minutes, then remove potatoes and brush the rest of your butter mixture over the tops and in the crevices. It should be easier this time around as the potato layers begin to separate!

7. Bake for another 30 minutes, or until the tops are crispy and middles are soft. Baking times may vary depending on the size of your potatoes.

8. Enjoy plain, or top with homemade vegan cheese sauce, pickled jalapeños, and freshly cracked black pepper, if desired.

fried green TOMATOES

A Southern classic that tastes delicious on its own, as a side dish, or on a sandwich. The movie *Fried Green Tomatoes* still makes my mom cry, even though she's seen it a thousand times. I hope she doesn't care that I just told everyone, but by now she's probably used to my big mouth. Also, there's nothing wrong with a good cry every now and then!

STUFF YOU NEED

Oil for frying (canola oil recommended)

¾   cup all-purpose flour

¾   cup cornmeal

1   tablespoon cornstarch

2   teaspoons freshly cracked black pepper

1   teaspoon salt

1   teaspoon garlic powder

1   cup plus 2 tablespoons unsweetened non-dairy milk (rice milk recommended)

3–4 large green tomatoes, sliced ½ inch thick

Dipping sauce: Rémoulade Sauce (page 185)

Recommended topping: sliced green onions

WHAT TO DO

1. If using a mini electric fryer, fill the fryer with oil and set the temperature to 375°F. To fry on the stovetop, review the important notes for success on page 21. For this recipe, you'll want to have at least 1 inch of oil in your frying pot.

2. While the oil is heating up, whisk together all dry ingredients in a large bowl. Add non-dairy milk and mix well with a spatula.

3. Once oil is at the right temperature, roll one of your green tomato slices around in the batter to fully coat. Use tongs to hold it up and rotate it so that the batter drips to cover the whole slice. If you have a few bare spots, it's fine. The batter will puff up in the frying oil.

4. Use a clean pair of heat-resistant tongs to gently grab the coated slice and transfer to the hot oil. Cook for 2–3 minutes, or until the batter is fluffy and golden brown.

5. Remove from the oil using a separate, clean pair of tongs and place on a paper towel-lined plate to absorb excess oil. Allow to cool before taste-testing.

6. If your slice was perfectly done, congratulations! Move on to the next step. If it had raw batter in the center or if the batter did not "fluff up" as expected, your oil is likely not hot enough. Try again with slightly increased heat, or try cooking the slice for an extra 30–60 seconds. If your batter is burnt...you probably know what to do here. Reduce your heat slightly, wait at least 5 minutes for the oil to cool, and try again.

7. Continue frying the rest of your slices in batches of 3–4, testing your oil temperature frequently for best results.

8. For maximum tastiness, serve immediately with homemade Rémoulade Sauce and sliced green onions.

baked home FRIES

Serves 4–6 **GF**

A healthier baked alternative to traditional Southern diner-style home fries, these little taters are a tasty side at breakfast or any time of day. Any of the homemade sauces in this book make a great dipping side, or just go with plain ol' ketchup.

STUFF YOU NEED

- 5   cups chopped russet potatoes (skin on, 1-inch pieces; about 2 large potatoes)
- 3   tablespoons olive oil
- 1   teaspoon minced garlic
- 1   teaspoon salt
- 1   teaspoon freshly cracked black pepper
- ½   teaspoon Krimsey's Cajun Seasoning (page 193)
- 1   tablespoon chopped fresh flat-leaf parsley

WHAT TO DO

1. Preheat oven to 400°F.

2. Place potatoes in a large mixing bowl and drizzle with olive oil. Add garlic and sprinkle with salt, pepper, and Cajun seasoning, then toss to coat.

3. Transfer potatoes to a baking sheet and spread out evenly. Bake for 20 minutes, then remove from the oven and stir. Return to the oven and bake for another 20 minutes.

4. Top with fresh parsley and serve.

crawfish boil CORN & POTATOES

Growing up, I liked to pick around the crawfish to try and find the prized potatoes. When a new crawfish batch came out (still scalding hot), I'd hastily dig for my precious potatoes, and my lack of patience always led to a burnt patch on the roof of my mouth. So worth it, though. I think? This recipe's all of the fun of the yummy potatoes without having to pick around the crawfish. To add your own spin on it, try experimenting with your favorite veggies (green beans, artichokes, brussels sprouts, etc.)!

STUFF YOU NEED

3   quarts water

¼   cup fresh lemon juice (about 2 medium lemons)

1   (3-ounce) box crab boil (I like Zatarain's brand)

2   tablespoons salt

2   teaspoons Krimsey's Cajun Seasoning (page 193)

¼   teaspoon cayenne pepper

1   medium yellow onion, quartered (outer layer removed)

1   whole head of garlic, unpeeled

2   pounds red potatoes, whole, scrubbed clean

6   frozen mini ears of corn

1   (8-ounce) package whole button mushrooms (or your favorite mushrooms)

Toppings: Krimsey's Cajun Seasoning (or freshly cracked black pepper) and lemon wedges

WHAT TO DO

1. Bring water, lemon juice, crab boil, salt, Cajun seasoning, cayenne pepper, onion, and garlic to a boil in an 8-quart pot, then drop in whole red potatoes.

2. Boil uncovered for about 20 minutes, or until potatoes start to get tender and can be fairly easily poked with a fork.

3. Drop in the frozen corn and mushrooms and wait for the water to boil again. Once boiling, cook for another 7–10 minutes, or until potatoes are cooked all the way through and mushrooms and corn are tender.

4. Scoop out veggies and serve! Top with Cajun seasoning (or freshly cracked black pepper) and lemon wedges for an authentic Louisiana feel. Try popping some of the garlic cloves once they've cooled, too—they're delicious.

TIP If you want that true, delicious, high-sodium crawfish boil taste, add up to 4 tablespoons of salt to your water. It sounds like a lot, and that's because it is. That's why I use 2 tablespoons. Remember, you're salting the water (not salting your food directly), so it's not as intense as it sounds.

one-pot mardi gras **MEDLEY**

Serves 2–3 **GF**

The green, purple, and yellow in this simple recipe (pictured on page 128) remind me of Mardi Gras and make getting my veggies in for the day so much easier. This recipe pairs well with the Blackened Cajun Tempeh (page 91) and the Yukon and Russet Mash (page 161).

STUFF YOU NEED

- 1½ cups baby brussels sprouts (about ½ pound), trimmed and cut in half
- 1 ear corn, shucked and cut crosswise into two or three pieces (or 2–3 frozen mini corn cobs)
- 1½ cups sliced red cabbage (about half a small cabbage), cut into 1-inch-wide strips
- 3 large kale leaves, hand-torn into chunks
  Juice of ½ small lemon (about 2 teaspoons)
- ½ teaspoon Krimsey's Cajun Seasoning (page 193), plus extra for topping

WHAT TO DO

1. Before starting, make sure you have all of your veggies chopped and ready to go. Note: Chopping through an ear of corn is no easy task. I suggest using a serrated knife to "saw" through it gently. You can chop the corn into as many pieces as you need depending on how many people you're serving.

2. Bring 1 inch of water to boil over medium-high heat in a 4-quart (or larger) pot with a lid.

3. Place brussels sprouts in a steamer basket insert and set over the boiling water. Cover and steam for 2 minutes.

4. Add corn cobs to the steamer basket, cover again, and cook for 2 minutes.

5. Add red cabbage to the steamer basket. Cover again and cook for another 2 minutes.

6. Add kale to the basket, cover, and steam for 1½ minutes more. When all the veggies are done cooking, they should be vibrant and colorful!

7. Remove the pot from the heat and take off the lid to stop the cooking process. Pour out the water from the main pot and transfer veggies out of the steamer basket into the dry pot.

8. Squeeze fresh lemon juice over veggies and sprinkle with Cajun seasoning. Use tongs to toss and distribute the flavors. Serve immediately, topped with additional Cajun seasoning if desired.

TIP Use fresh-picked farmers' market veggies for maximum flavor. It really does make a difference!

sweet & salty cast-iron **CORNBREAD**

Makes 1 (10-inch) skillet; serves 6–8

There's nothing like a fresh, warm slice of old-fashioned cornbread with butter to zap you back to simpler days. This Southern classic is the perfect mix of salty and sweet. Share it with a few folks if you want to make new friends, or save it all for yourself (no one is watching, and FYI, it freezes well!). Note: If you don't have a cast-iron skillet, you can use a regular 9×9-inch baking pan, a 10-inch round pan, or even a muffin pan instead. Just skip the skillet preheating step and follow the other instructions as usual. If you are working with a pan larger or smaller than recommended, just be aware that you might need to shorten or lengthen the baking time slightly to account for the difference in batter depth. (A bigger pan will produce a thinner cornbread that needs less baking time, and vice versa.)

STUFF YOU NEED

1⅓ cups all-purpose flour

1 cup cornmeal

½ cup plus 1 tablespoon cane sugar

2 teaspoons baking powder

2 teaspoons salt

1⅓ cups unsweetened non-dairy milk (rice milk recommended)

⅓ cup plus ½ tablespoon vegan butter, divided

1½ tablespoons maple syrup

Recommended toppings: Maple Hunny Butter (page 188), vegan butter, and/or peanut butter

WHAT TO DO

1. Place a 10-inch pre-seasoned cast-iron skillet in the oven (see page 18 for tips on seasoning) and preheat to 375°F. This will allow the cast iron to heat up slowly and evenly while you prepare your batter. If you're not using cast iron, just preheat the oven to 375°F.

2. In a large bowl, whisk together flour, cornmeal, sugar, baking powder, and salt.

3. When well combined, use a spatula to mix in non-dairy milk, ⅓ cup of melted vegan butter, and maple syrup. Gently blend until chunks are gone.

4. Once your oven is heated and your batter is ready to go, use an oven mitt to carefully remove your cast-iron skillet from the oven. Place it on a flat, level surface with a towel or trivet beneath to protect the surface from heat.

5. Add remaining ½ tablespoon vegan butter to your hot cast-iron skillet and tilt to spread it around the bottom of the pan as it melts. If you're not using cast iron, coat your pan with a thin layer of vegan butter (baking spray or lining the pan with parchment paper works too, but it's not quite as tasty).

(Recipe continues on next page)

(Recipe continued from previous page)

6. Use a spatula to scrape all batter from the mixing bowl into the hot skillet, being careful to avoid splashing the sizzling butter or accidentally touching the hot pan. Pour into the center and let the batter creep to the edges of the pan evenly. If needed, use your spatula to smooth out the top of the batter— it may need a little coaxing to fall evenly.

7. Return the batter-filled skillet to the oven and bake for 35–40 minutes, or until the top of your cornbread is light golden brown with dark edges and darker spots throughout. The cornbread will continue to cook for a few minutes after removing it from the oven, so err on the lighter side.

8. Serve warm with a side of Maple Hunny Butter, vegan butter, and/or peanut butter (hey, don't knock it 'til you've tried it!).

southern HUSHPUPPIES

There are tons of theories out there on how hushpuppies came about, and who knows how they were "really" born. However, my favorite story involves dogs. The story goes that soldiers used to feed their begging dogs fried cornbread to make them hush during cookouts. I get it: these pups make me hush too, especially if I've got Cajun Ranch to dip them in.

STUFF YOU NEED

Oil for frying (canola oil recommended)

1   cup cornmeal

⅔   cup flour

1   tablespoon cane sugar

2   teaspoons salt

1   teaspoon baking powder

¼   teaspoon cayenne pepper

1   cup unsweetened non-dairy milk (rice milk recommended)

¼   cup vegetable oil

1   teaspoon Tabasco sauce

½   cup corn kernels, fresh or frozen

½   cup diced yellow onion

1   jalapeño, finely diced, optional

Dipping sauce: Cajun Ranch (page 181)
Special tool: No. 40 (0.86-ounce) food scooper

WHAT TO DO

1. If using a mini electric fryer, fill the fryer with oil and set the temperature to 350°F. To fry on the stovetop, review the important notes for success on page 21. For this recipe, you'll want to have at least 1½ inches of oil in your frying pot. While the oil is heating, mix up your batter.

2. In a large bowl, whisk together cornmeal, flour, sugar, salt, baking powder, and cayenne pepper.

3. Slowly add non-dairy milk, vegetable oil, and Tabasco sauce. Once well blended, gently beat in corn, onion, and jalapeño, if using.

4. Once oil is at right temperature, use a small food scooper with a release button (recommended) or a tablespoon measuring spoon to drop a 1-inch ball of batter into the hot frying oil. Be careful to drop it as close to the oil as possible (you don't want it to fall and splash into the oil, you want it to glide in). Cook for 3–4 minutes, or until the outside is golden brown. Remove from oil using tongs or a frying strainer, then place on a paper towel-lined plate. Let cool for a minute, then cut the hushpuppy open to make sure it's cooked all the way through. If it's raw in the middle, you probably need to turn the frying temp up, so make sure you're actually at 350°F. Even 5°F lower could cause problems!

5. Continue with the rest of your pups, and let cool slightly before serving with Cajun Ranch.

TIP This batter can be prepared ahead of time and refrigerated for up to 24 hours. You can fry i mmediately; it doesn't need to be brought to room temperature first.

kale & tempeh'd **BLACK-EYED PEAS**

When I first discovered tempeh, I was so confused. Is it peanuts? It looks kind of moldy…is this normal? How do I cook it? A decade later, it's one of my favorite plant-based meat replacements. It's definitely not meat (no confusion there), but it's hearty and protein-packed with a yummy nutty flavor. It's also minimally processed, so the original nutrients mostly remain intact. I like to enhance its flavor by cooking in broth or stock, and choosing to add kale and black-eyed peas is just a natural extension of my crunchy granola-Southern-vegan-hippie desires.

STUFF YOU NEED

- 2 tablespoons olive oil
- 1 cup diced yellow onion (about 1 medium onion)
- 1 (8-ounce) package tempeh, crumbled
- 1 tablespoon minced garlic
- 1½ cups cooked black-eyed peas (or about one 15-ounce can, drained)
- ½ bunch curly kale, shredded (about 2 cups packed)
- 1 cup low-sodium vegetable stock
- 3 tablespoons soy sauce (or Bragg liquid aminos)
- 2 teaspoons brown sugar
- ½ teaspoon freshly cracked black pepper
- ¼ teaspoon salt, or to taste
- ⅛ teaspoon liquid smoke

Topping: freshly cracked black pepper

WHAT TO DO

1. Heat oil in a 3-quart pot over medium heat.

2. Add diced onion and crumbled tempeh and cook uncovered for 5–7 minutes, or until onion begins to look translucent and tempeh has some brown edges. Stir only once per minute. Add garlic and stir frequently for another 2–3 minutes until browned.

3. Add black-eyed peas, kale, vegetable stock, soy sauce, brown sugar, black pepper, salt, and liquid smoke. Mix well and bring to a gentle simmer, then reduce heat to medium-low. Add shredded kale and cook until kale is just barely wilted, about 1–2 minutes.

4. Top with freshly cracked black pepper and serve.

louisiana **COLLARD GREENS**

Serves 4–6 **GF**

As with many other delicious and well-known Southern recipes, African slaves in the South originally introduced this dish to Louisiana. Plantation owners would give them leftover food scraps (including greens and meat leftovers), and the ingenious and resourceful African cooks found a way to make them delicious by boiling the collards with things like ham hocks and various spices. Collards grow quickly during Southern winters, so they were readily available and used often.

STUFF YOU NEED

3   tablespoons olive oil

1   cup thinly sliced onion (about 1 medium onion)

1   tablespoon minced garlic

4   cups low-sodium vegetable stock

2   tablespoons apple cider vinegar

1   teaspoon Bragg liquid aminos, or soy sauce (regular or gluten-free)

2   teaspoons Krimsey's Cajun Seasoning (page 193)

1   teaspoon brown sugar

1   teaspoon salt, plus extra for topping

½   teaspoon freshly cracked black pepper

¼   teaspoon crushed red pepper

¼   teaspoon liquid smoke

⅛   teaspoon ground bay leaf (or 1 whole bay leaf)

2   bunches collard greens (about 10 stems total), washed, de-stemmed, and sliced into 1-inch strips

Topping: Smoky Maple Bacon Bits (page 196)

WHAT TO DO

1. Heat olive oil in a 4-quart pot over medium heat. Add onions and cook, only stirring 2–3 times, for 8–10 minutes to caramelize.

2. Add garlic and cook for another minute.

3. Add vegetable stock, apple cider vinegar, liquid aminos, Cajun seasoning, brown sugar, salt, black pepper, crushed red pepper, liquid smoke, and bay leaf.

4. Bring to a soft boil, then add collards. Lower the heat to medium-low, cover, and simmer for about 40 minutes, or until collards are tender.

5. Add salt to taste, portion into bowls, top with Smoky Maple Bacon Bits, and serve.

green bean CASSEROLE

Serves 8–12 **GF**

Thanksgiving is an odd holiday to me, but I do love hanging with family and friends and tasting all the delicious treats that everyone made at home. This is a recipe that I typically only make once per year, because it just feels wrong to eat green bean casserole on any other day. I won't say this recipe is "difficult," but it does require some time and love (trimming green beans is tedious). I invite you to slow down and enjoy the process.

STUFF YOU NEED

1½ pounds fresh green beans, trimmed and cut into 1½-inch pieces

1 teaspoon salt, divided

1 cup low-sodium vegetable stock

1 cup unsweetened non-dairy milk (rice milk recommended)

⅓ cup nutritional yeast

¼ cup all-purpose flour (for gluten-free, use 1/8 cup rice flour instead)

1 tablespoon Bragg liquid aminos, or soy sauce (regular or gluten-free)

½ teaspoon freshly cracked black pepper

2 tablespoons olive oil

1 cup diced onion

1 (8-ounce) package sliced mushrooms

3 garlic cloves, minced

1 teaspoon dried thyme

1 (3-ounce) can French fried onions (or gluten-free version)

½ teaspoon paprika

WHAT TO DO

1. Bring a pot of water to boil, then add green beans and ½ teaspoon salt. Cook 10–15 minutes, or until beans are bright green and slightly crunchy. Drain well and set aside.

2. Preheat oven to 375°F. In a large bowl, whisk together vegetable stock, non-dairy milk, nutritional yeast, flour, liquid aminos, ½ teaspoon salt, and black pepper. Set aside.

3. Heat oil in a large skillet or pot over medium heat. Add onion and cook for 5–7 minutes, stirring occasionally until slightly softened, then add mushrooms, garlic, and thyme. Cook until mushrooms get juicy, about 5 minutes.

4. Add the vegetable stock mixture to the mushrooms and simmer until the liquid thickens, about 10 minutes.

5. Lightly oil a 9×13-inch (or 12-inch round) casserole dish and add cooked green beans. Pour mushroom broth mixture over the beans. Mix gently to coat the beans, then cover the casserole dish with a lid or foil and bake for 20 minutes.

6. Remove the lid, sprinkle French fried onions and paprika over the top, and return to the oven to bake for another 10–15 minutes. The dish is ready when it's brown, bubbly, and slightly crispy in some places. Let cool slightly and serve.

simple ARTICHOKES

There's something really zany and quirky about eating artichoke leaves straight off the plant. It's like eating alien food. When I make these for others, they are usually unfamiliar with how to eat them, so this is a great conversation piece! I am shocked by how many people haven't eaten artichokes this way, which is why I chose to include this simple recipe even though it's not very Cajun. If you dip it in Rémoulade Sauce, though, like magic, it's officially a Cajun dish.

STUFF YOU NEED

2   small artichokes, sharp tips cut off
    of each leaf
    Juice of 1 large lemon

2   large garlic cloves, whole

½   teaspoon salt

Dipping sauce: Rémoulade Sauce, page 185 (or mustard works, too)

WHAT TO DO

1. Fill a 4-quart pot with water and bring to a boil.

2. Add artichokes, lemon juice, garlic, and salt.

3. Boil gently for 45 minutes over medium-high heat, turning artichokes over in the water halfway through.

4. While artichokes are boiling, make Rémoulade Sauce and chill until ready to serve. If you don't feel like mixing dip, just use mustard. It totally works here.

5. To eat: Pull a leaf from the artichoke and bite into the meaty part. Pull back the meat using your teeth, and leave the tough leaf behind.

TIP Cut the cooked artichokes in half (through the stem) to help them cool faster.

loaded jalapeño CORNBREAD MUFFINS

Despite the "jalapeño" in the name, these cornbread muffins aren't too spicy. They carry the jalapeño flavor, but not the heat. If you like food that bites back, try subbing in habanero peppers for the jalapeño peppers.

STUFF YOU NEED

1½ cups cornmeal

1½ cups all-purpose flour

¾ cup cane sugar

2 teaspoons baking powder

2 teaspoons salt

1¾ cups unsweetened non-dairy milk
    (rice milk recommended)

½ cup vegan butter, melted

1 jalapeño, deseeded and finely diced
    (3–4 tablespoons diced)

½ cup finely diced yellow onion

½ cup corn kernels, fresh or canned
    (well drained)

¾ cup vegan cheddar cheese shreds

Topping: vegan cheddar cheese shreds
and coarse-ground salt

For serving: vegan butter

WHAT TO DO

1. Preheat your oven to 375°F.

2. In a large bowl, whisk together cornmeal, flour, sugar, baking powder, and salt.

3. When well combined, use a spatula to mix in non-dairy milk and melted butter. Gently blend until chunks are gone.

4. Set aside about 1 tablespoon of diced jalapeño for topping, then fold in the rest of the diced jalapeño, yellow onion, corn, and vegan cheese.

5. Transfer batter to a lightly oiled 12-cup muffin pan. If using a standard-sized muffin pan, you should fill each cup almost to the very top—don't be afraid of overflow! Filling them this high will make big, beautiful muffin tops.

6. Sprinkle a bit of vegan cheese and diced jalapeño on each raw muffin, then grind a tiny bit of coarse salt on top.

7. Bake for 30 minutes, or until muffin tops turn golden brown.

8. Let cool slightly and serve warm with vegan butter.

 *smothered* **OKRA**

Okra contains fiber, potassium, vitamin B, vitamin C, folic acid, and calcium. But that's not why I eat it...I just like stuff that lights up my taste buds. I enjoy this one over fluffy parboiled rice. It's not a super cute-looking dish (how do you make okra mush cute?), but it redeems itself with flavor.

STUFF YOU NEED

6   cups chopped fresh okra (or 24 ounces frozen okra, thawed and drained

1   cup thinly sliced yellow onion (about ½ large onion)

1   cup diced red bell pepper (about 1 medium pepper)

¼   cup vegan butter

1   (14.5-ounce) can diced tomatoes, with juice

2½ teaspoons Krimsey's Cajun Seasoning (page 193)

2   teaspoons minced garlic

½   teaspoon salt

½   teaspoon freshly cracked black pepper, plus extra for topping

WHAT TO DO

1. Preheat the oven to 375°F.

2. Combine okra, yellow onion, and red bell pepper in a lightly-oiled 9×13-inch casserole dish.

3. In a separate bowl, mix melted vegan butter, diced tomatoes and their juice, Cajun seasoning, garlic, salt, and black pepper. Spoon mixture on top of the okra and veggies in your casserole dish.

4. Use tongs to mix well, then cover the dish with a lid or foil and bake for 1 hour. After 1 hour, uncover and bake for another 20 minutes.

5. Remove from the oven and top with freshly cracked black pepper. Serve hot.

cranberry pecan COLESLAW

This is what I would call "fancy slaw." It's like when regular slaw puts on Sunday church clothes. This side dish gets a touch of sweetness from the maple syrup, and a bit of tart from the cranberries and apple cider vinegar. Hallelujah, praise be!

STUFF YOU NEED

½ cup vegan mayo

1 tablespoon apple cider vinegar

1 tablespoon maple syrup

1 teaspoon salt

1 teaspoon freshly cracked black pepper

2 cups shredded green cabbage

1 cup shredded red cabbage

½ cup shredded carrots

2 tablespoons thinly sliced green onions

1 cup hand-crushed pecans

¾ cup dried, unsweetened cranberries

WHAT TO DO

1. In a large bowl, whisk together vegan mayo, apple cider vinegar, maple syrup, salt, and black pepper.

2. Toss in green and red shredded cabbage, carrots, green onions, crushed pecans, and dried cranberries. Use tongs to mix and evenly coat all ingredients.

3. Serve immediately, or let sit in the fridge for a couple of hours if you prefer a wetter and softer slaw.

black sheep SLAW

If my Granny were alive, I think she'd probably think it was super rad that I moved to California, got tattooed, and botched a classic Southern coleslaw recipe in such a way. And although she'd probably be confused about why I chose to shave my head, she'd still secretly think that was super cool, too.

STUFF YOU NEED

⅓ cup vegan mayo

2 tablespoons yellow mustard

1 tablespoon cane sugar

2 teaspoons apple cider vinegar

1 teaspoon unsulphured molasses

½ teaspoon salt

½ teaspoon freshly cracked black pepper

½ teaspoon paprika

½ teaspoon Krimsey's Cajun Seasoning (page 193)

Pinch of cayenne pepper, optional

3½ cups shredded green cabbage

⅓ cup shredded red cabbage

¼ cup shredded carrots

2 tablespoons thinly sliced green onion

Topping: freshly cracked black pepper

WHAT TO DO

1. In a large bowl, whisk together vegan mayo, mustard, sugar, apple cider vinegar, molasses, salt, black pepper, paprika, Cajun seasoning, and cayenne pepper, if using.

2. Toss in green and red cabbage, carrots, and green onion, then use tongs to mix and coat thoroughly.

3. Let sit in the fridge for at least an hour before serving to let the cabbage soften and the flavors blend. (It will start to turn pink after a few hours, but it's still delicious.) Top with freshly cracked black pepper and serve.

tangy brussels sprout SLAW

There are a lot of things going on here. The combination of all of the sweet, salty, and tangy flavors creates a new and unique salad that's pretty quick to whip up when you're looking for something new to break up the monotony of eating mostly potatoes (or is that just me?). I use the core of my brussels sprouts along with the leaves, but if the core bothers you, just shred around it.

STUFF YOU NEED

- 2 tablespoons olive oil
- 2 tablespoons Dijon mustard
- 1 tablespoon maple syrup
- 1 tablespoon fresh lemon juice
- 1 tablespoon vegan parmesan cheese crumbles
- 1½ teaspoons balsamic vinaigrette
- ¼ teaspoon salt
- ½ teaspoon freshly cracked black pepper
- 1 pound brussels sprouts, shredded
- 1½ cups shredded red cabbage
- 1 medium apple, diced (Gala recommended)
- ¾ cup roasted whole cashews

Toppings: vegan parmesan cheese crumbles and freshly cracked black pepper

WHAT TO DO

1. In a medium bowl, whisk together olive oil, Dijon mustard, maple syrup, lemon juice, vegan parmesan cheese crumbles, balsamic vinaigrette, salt, and black pepper.

2. Add shredded brussels sprouts, red cabbage, apple, and roasted cashews. Use tongs to toss and coat evenly.

3. Transfer to individual serving bowls, and top with more vegan parmesan cheese and freshly cracked black pepper.

Krimfession Time...

When my mom made this recipe, she loved it, but also asked, "Why didn't you use peanuts instead of cashews?" Gee, mom, not sure. Because that's what I like? But I thought I'd include her feedback in case peanuts sound better to you, too.

TIP To save time, you can make the dressing and prep the veggies up to 24 hours in advance, but wait until the last minute to combine everything. Otherwise, it will get soggy—still delicious, but less fun to look at.

cajun **POTATO WEDGES**

Makes as many as you want! **GF**

This was my favorite menu item at the restaurant. I loved getting a big Bayou Goddess Bowl (page 121) and scarfing it with a side of wedges and Cajun Ranch. I mean, they're whole foods so they're good for you.

I didn't include quantities for ingredients here, because you can just make as much as you want. As a rule of thumb, I recommend approximately ½ teaspoon of Cajun seasoning for every 6 wedges.

STUFF YOU NEED

Oil for frying (canola oil recommended)

Russet potatoes

Krimsey's Cajun Seasoning (page 193)

Dipping sauce: Cajun Ranch (page 181)

WHAT TO DO

1. If using a mini electric fryer, fill the fryer with oil and set the temperature to 375°F. To fry on the stovetop, review the important notes for success on page 21. For this recipe, you'll want to have at least 1½ inches of oil in your frying pot.

2. While the oil is heating, prepare your potatoes. Wash and scrub them, then slice each potato in half lengthwise. Place potatoes cut-side down on the cutting board and slice each potato half into 3–4 wedges. They should be about 1 inch wide at the fattest parts.

3. When oil is at right temperature, use heat-resistant tongs to carefully place a couple of tester wedges in the fryer or pot and cook for 4–5 minutes, or until outsides are light golden brown and they're beginning to get tender, but are not yet fully cooked. The cook time will depend heavily on the size of potatoes used. Remove and let cool for at least 5 minutes on a paper towel-lined plate, then give them another 2–3 minutes in the fryer. When fully cooked, they should be golden brown with crispy outsides.

4. Use tongs to transfer wedges back to the paper towel-lined plate for another minute to cool down. Then, transfer to a small bowl and sprinkle with as much Cajun seasoning as desired. Flip and toss to coat.

5. Taste test, and if wedges are undercooked or overcooked, adjust the cook time accordingly. I recommend adjusting the cook time during the first fryer dip, rather than the last fryer dip, since the final dip is mostly for crisping the outsides (not cooking the insides). Continue frying the rest of your wedges in small batches.

6. Serve immediately with Cajun Ranch dipping sauce.

fried DILL PICKLES

Makes 12–15 spears or 20–30 chips (depending on the size of the spears/chips you're using!)

You can use pickle spears or chips for this recipe. If you opt for pickle chips, they'll be much more flavor-intense because there's more surface area to cover in batter. So go for the chips if you're a salt and vinegar lover, and the spears if you prefer a milder experience. If you're a first-time fryer, be careful! Because the batter is liquidy, it's somewhat of an advanced frying recipe. So just be aware that the oil may spray out a bit—always use the longest tongs you can to protect yourself from the sizzling oil.

STUFF YOU NEED

Frying oil (canola recommended)

¾ cup all-purpose flour

¼ cup cornmeal

¼ cup cornstarch

2 teaspoons freshly cracked black pepper

1 teaspoon paprika

1 teaspoon garlic powder

1 teaspoon onion powder

1 teaspoon salt

½ teaspoon chili powder

⅛ teaspoon cayenne pepper

1 cup cold water

Dill pickles (12–15 spears, or 20–30 chips)

Topping: vegan parmesan cheese crumbles

Dipping sauce: Cajun Ranch (page 181)

WHAT TO DO

1. If using a mini electric fryer, fill the fryer with oil and set the temperature to 375°F. To fry on the stovetop, review the important notes for success on page 21. For this recipe, you'll want to have at least 1 inch of oil in your frying pot. While the oil is heating, mix up your batter.

2. In a large bowl, whisk together flour, cornmeal, cornstarch, black pepper, paprika, garlic powder, onion powder, salt, chili powder, and cayenne pepper. Once well combined, mix in cold water with a spatula or large spoon. The batter may feel a little more liquidy than a standard wet batter, but it's on purpose.

3. When oil is at right temperature, use tongs to dip one pickle spear or chip into the batter (no need to dry the pickles off first), then wiggle it to knock off any dripping batter. Quickly transfer into the hot oil. Because the batter is so liquidy, it could cause the oil to pop a little more than usual, so be careful when dropping it in. Fry for 2–3 minutes, or until the batter is golden brown.

4. When finished cooking, use tongs to transfer them to a paper towel-lined plate to cool slightly.

5. Taste test. If your fried pickle is perfectly done, congratulations! Move on to the next step. If it did not form a solid golden-brown crust as expected, your oil is likely not hot enough. Try again with slightly increased heat, or try cooking the pickles for an extra 30–60 seconds. If your batter is burnt... you probably know what to do here. Reduce your heat slightly, wait at least 5 minutes for the oil to cool, and try again.

6. Continue frying the rest of your pickles in small batches and transfer them to the paper towel-lined plate when done to cool slightly.

7. Top with vegan parmesan cheese and serve immediately with Cajun Ranch dipping sauce.

fried OKRA

Serves 2–4 (makes about 2½ cups)

It's easy to eat all of these before you're actually ready to sit down at the table and enjoy the rest of your meal. So perhaps you should treat fried okra more like popcorn—a food best enjoyed by the handful as a crunchy snack independent of dinner.

STUFF YOU NEED

Oil for frying (canola recommended)

2 cups frozen cut okra (about ½ pound)

⅓ cup cornmeal

¼ cup all-purpose flour

1½ teaspoons cane sugar

1½ teaspoons cornstarch

1 teaspoon salt

½ teaspoon freshly cracked black pepper

½ teaspoon baking powder

½ teaspoon garlic powder

⅛ teaspoon cayenne pepper

Dipping sauce: Cajun Ranch (page 181)

WHAT TO DO

1. If using a mini electric fryer, fill the fryer with oil and set the temperature to 375°F. To fry on the stovetop, review the important notes for success on page 21. For this recipe, you'll want to have at least 1 inch of oil in your frying pot. While the oil is heating, prepare the okra and mix up your batter.

2. In a medium bowl, cover frozen okra with hot water and allow it to defrost.

3. In a large bowl, whisk together cornmeal, flour, sugar, cornstarch, salt, black pepper, baking powder, garlic powder, and cayenne pepper. Set aside.

4. When oil is at right temperature, use tongs to lift a few pieces of defrosted okra out of the water, squeeze out excess water, and transfer to the dry batter bowl. Stir and toss to coat, then use a slotted spoon to sift out battered okra pieces and drop into the hot frying oil.

5. Fry for 2–3 minutes, or until the batter is crispy and light golden brown. When finished cooking, use a slotted spoon to move them to a paper towel-lined plate to cool slightly.

6. Taste test. If your fried okra is perfectly done, congratulations! Move on to the next step. If your batter did not create a crispy golden-brown crust as expected, your oil is likely not hot enough. Try again with slightly increased heat, or try cooking for an extra 30–60 seconds. If your batter is burnt...you probably know what to do here. Reduce your heat slightly, wait at least 5 minutes for the oil to cool, and try again.

7. Continue frying the rest of your okra in small batches and transfer them to the paper towel-lined plate when done to cool slightly.

8. Serve immediately with Cajun Ranch dipping sauce.

dill POTATO SALAD

Bring this to your next potluck—I guarantee it will be a hit. The fresh dill adds something unique and interesting to a dish that is classically delicious, and the diced celery and onions come in clutch with some crunch. This was one of my favorite sides at my North Hollywood restaurant.

STUFF YOU NEED

2½ pounds red potatoes, chopped into 1-inch pieces (6 cups chopped)

3½ teaspoons salt, divided

1   cup vegan mayo

¾   cup diced celery (about 1 stalk)

½   cup diced white onion

3   tablespoons dill pickle relish

2   tablespoons chopped fresh dill

2   tablespoons yellow mustard

1½ teaspoons freshly cracked black pepper

1   tablespoon chopped fresh parsley

Toppings: fresh parsley and freshly cracked black pepper

WHAT TO DO

1. Place chopped potatoes in a large pot, cover with water, and add 2 teaspoons of salt. Bring to a boil over medium-high heat. Once water starts boiling, reduce heat to medium and boil gently for 10 minutes.

2. Meanwhile, in a small bowl, combine vegan mayo, celery, onion, dill pickle relish, fresh dill, yellow mustard, 1½ teaspoons of salt, black pepper, and fresh parsley. Set aside in the fridge.

3. After 10 minutes, pierce one of the potatoes with a fork. If you can easily pierce it through the middle, they're done. Drain off the water immediately, transfer potatoes to a large bowl, and allow them to cool completely. To accelerate the cooling process, stick them in the fridge! If you try to finish this dish while the potatoes are still even slightly warm, you'll melt the mayo and you'll regret it.

4. When potatoes are completely cooled, add vegan mayo mixture to the bowl and toss to coat. Use a potato masher or sturdy spoon to smoosh the potatoes until you have reached your desired level of chunkiness. You probably don't want to go full "mashed potato," but it's your party so you can do what you want.

5. Top with fresh parsley and freshly cracked black pepper. Serve and enjoy!

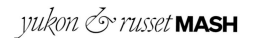

yukon & russet **MASH**

Yukons are soft and creamy, and russets are light and fluffy. Together, they're a magical pair. This recipe makes a thick and slightly sticky batch of taters, so if you like them thinner, just add more non-dairy milk, ¼ cup at a time.

STUFF YOU NEED

- 4 cups chopped Yukon gold potatoes (skin on, about 1½ pounds)
- 4 cups chopped russet potatoes (skin on, about 2 pounds)
- 3 teaspoons salt, divided
- 2 garlic cloves, thinly sliced
- ⅓ cup vegan butter, melted
- ½ cup unsweetened non-dairy milk, warmed (rice milk recommended)
- 1 teaspoon garlic powder
- ½ teaspoon freshly cracked black pepper

Toppings: Smoky Maple Bacon Bits (page 196), sliced green onions, and paprika or Krimsey's Cajun Seasoning (page 193)

WHAT TO DO

1. Place all potatoes in a medium pot and cover with water. Add 1½ teaspoons of salt and the sliced garlic, then cover and bring to a boil over medium-high heat.

2. When water starts boiling, reduce heat to medium and boil (lid on) for 10–12 minutes, or until a fork easily pokes through potatoes. (If your pot lid doesn't have a vent hole, then tilt the lid slightly to let steam out so it doesn't boil over.) Once potatoes are tender, remove from the heat and pour into a colander to drain off water.

3. Return potatoes to the pot. While potatoes are still hot, stir in vegan butter and warm non-dairy milk, remaining 1½ teaspoons of salt, garlic powder, and black pepper. Use a potato masher (or a sturdy spoon) to smash up potatoes and blend in liquids. The butter should melt as you mix. If you prefer a wetter mash, add a little extra non-dairy milk until you're happy with what you've created.

4. Stir in garlic powder, remaining 1 teaspoon salt, and black pepper.

5. Top with Smoky Maple Bacon Bits, sliced green opinions, and paprika or Cajun seasoning and serve immediately.

dirty **RICE**

Makes about 6 cups **GF**

A distant, slightly less complicated side-dish cousin to jambalaya, dirty rice is a Cajun classic. The name comes from the "dirty" appearance of the rice due to the brown specks of ground meat. Using the "Holy Trinity" (celery, bell pepper, onion) as a base creates a really authentic and recognizable Louisiana flavor. I like to use long-grain white rice here (instead of my go-to parboiled rice), because it's truer to the taste and texture of what I grew up on. However, it's less forgiving, so watch it closely while cooking so you don't wind up with mush.

STUFF YOU NEED

- 1 tablespoon vegan butter
- 1 cup diced white onion (about 1 medium onion)
- 1 cup diced green bell pepper (about 1 medium pepper)
- 1 cup diced celery (about 2 stalks)
- 1 tablespoon minced garlic
- 1½ cups low-sodium vegetable stock, plus extra as needed
- 1½ cups water
- 1½ cups dry long-grain white rice
- 1½ teaspoons salt
- 1½ teaspoons freshly cracked black pepper
- 1 teaspoon dried thyme
- 1 teaspoon paprika
- ⅛ teaspoon cayenne pepper, or ¼ teaspoon for spice lovers
- 2 bay leaves
- 2 cups frozen vegan beef crumbles (or gluten-free version)

Toppings: sliced green onions and fresh parsley

WHAT TO DO

1. Heat vegan butter in a 4-quart pot over medium heat and add onion, bell pepper, and celery. Cook for 4 minutes, stirring occasionally until onions begin to look translucent. Add garlic and cook for another 2 minutes.

2. Add vegetable stock, water, rice, salt, black pepper, thyme, paprika, cayenne pepper, and bay leaves. Bring to a boil, then reduce the heat and simmer, covered, for 8 minutes. Remove from the heat, stir, and re-cover. Let steam off the heat for 7 more minutes. Do not open the lid during this process.

3. Return to low heat and add vegan beef crumbles. Heat just until warm throughout. Note: If the rice doesn't feel done when you add the crumbles, add another ⅓ cup vegetable stock and increase the heat to medium. Simmer for another 3–5 minutes, watching the rice carefully. It can go from underdone to overdone mush in a matter of minutes.

4. Serve topped with sliced green onions and fresh parsley.

deviled red **POTATOES**

Makes 1 dozen **GF**

When I was a kid at Christmas parties, I ate deviled eggs until I got sick. I was also one of those weird kids that really enjoyed egg salad and tuna fish sandwiches (plain). I've sort of grown out of that phase, but I'm still a sucker for simple recipes done well—like this one—that remind me of the big family gatherings I attended in my youth.

STUFF YOU NEED

12 small red potatoes (about the size of an egg)

¼ cup vegan mayo

2 tablespoons yellow mustard

2 tablespoons dill pickle relish

¼ teaspoon salt

½ teaspoon freshly cracked black pepper

Toppings: paprika, sliced chives, salt, and freshly cracked black pepper

WHAT TO DO

1. Wash and scrub red potatoes, then slice in half and place in a steamer basket. This recipe makes a dozen deviled potatoes, but we're steaming some extras just in case you need more.

2. In a medium pot that will hold your steamer basket, bring 1 inch of water to a boil, then insert the basket of potatoes. Cover and steam for 16–18 minutes, or until potatoes are cooked all the way through. Allow potatoes to cool completely before proceeding.

3. Once potatoes are cool, use a melon baller or spoon to remove one scoop of the insides of 24 potato halves and transfer them to a medium bowl. Set the skins aside. Mash potato insides with a potato masher or sturdy spoon. You should end up with about a cup of potato mash—if you don't, throw in the insides from some of those extra potatoes to make a full cup. Have leftover potatoes? Enjoy the snack!

4. Add the vegan mayo, mustard, pickle relish, salt, and black pepper to your cup of potato mash. Mix thoroughly using a handheld electric mixer if you have one; otherwise a fork and spoon will do.

5. If you have a star icing tip, insert it into a piping bag or plastic sandwich bag. (If you don't, you can just use a plastic bag with a corner cut off.) Transfer the potato-mayo mix to the bag and pipe into your potato skins.

6. Sprinkle tops with paprika, sliced chives, salt, and freshly cracked black pepper.

7. Serve chilled or at room temperature—they're delicious either way!

atchafalaya corn STIR-FRY

Serves 4–6 (makes about 5 cups) **GF**

A nod to the classic Louisiana Corn Maque Choux dish, this side dish works best with fresh corn off the cob. It's named after the Atchafalaya Basin, the largest swamp in the United States. Most people assume the Florida Everglades are the biggest wetlands, but this Louisiana "secret" is home to about sixty-five species of reptiles and amphibians.

STUFF YOU NEED

- 2 teaspoons olive oil
- 2 links vegan sausage, diced (spicy recommended; can also use gluten-free version)
- 3 cups fresh corn kernels (recommended), or canned (well-drained)
- 1 cup diced yellow onion (about 1 small onion)
- 1 cup diced red bell pepper (about 1 small bell pepper)
- 1 finely diced jalapeño (about 3 tablespoons)
- 2 teaspoons minced garlic
- 1 tablespoon Krimsey's Cajun Seasoning (page 193)
- 1 teaspoon salt
- 1 teaspoon freshly cracked black pepper, plus extra for topping
- ¼ cup sliced green onions

WHAT TO DO

1. Heat olive oil in a large, deep saucepan over medium-high heat. Add vegan sausage and sauté for 4–5 minutes, or until edges begin to brown.

2. Add corn, onion, red bell pepper, jalapeño, and garlic. Raise heat to high and cook, stirring infrequently, for 6–8 minutes, or until onion becomes translucent. Stir only once per minute or two to encourage browning on the bottom of the pan.

3. Add Cajun seasoning, salt, and black pepper and cook for another 2–3 minutes.

4. Remove from the heat and stir in green onions.

5. Top with freshly cracked black pepper and serve.

"almost dessert" twice-baked **SWEET POTATOES**

I struggled with whether to call this dish a "side" or a "dessert," but it's mostly potato, so I think it counts as a vegetable. Sweet potatoes are filled with good-for-you nutrients, which basically balance out all the added sugar. (Sort of.)

STUFF YOU NEED

4 medium sweet potatoes (about 1 pound each), washed and scrubbed

4 teaspoons vegan butter

1 tablespoon brown sugar

½ teaspoon ground cinnamon

½ teaspoon salt

½ cup vegan chocolate chips, divided

½ cup vegan mini marshmallows, divided

¼ cup crumbled pecans

1 tablespoon shredded coconut

WHAT TO DO

1. Preheat oven to 375°F.

2. Pierce each sweet potato with a fork 2–3 times. Place potatoes on a baking sheet and bake for 1 hour, or until a fork can be poked through to the center and potatoes begin bubbling out some juices. Larger potatoes will take longer, of course. Set aside to cool until they can be handled (leave the oven on).

3. Once cooled, carefully split the sweet potatoes lengthwise down the center and squeeze at the ends to open up the potato. Use a fork to remove the orange flesh inside. Transfer the insides to a medium bowl and stir in vegan butter, brown sugar, cinnamon, and salt. Add ¼ cup vegan chocolate chips and ¼ cup mini marshmallows, then return the mashed potato mixture to the potato skins.

4. Top with remaining ¼ cup mini marshmallows and ¼ cup vegan chocolate chips, as well as the pecans and shredded coconut, dividing toppings evenly among potatoes.

5. Bake for another 15 minutes, then remove from the oven and allow to cool slightly before enjoying.

Smoked Chili Cheeze Sauce

Dressings, Sauces,
& TOPPINGS

sweet chili BBQ SAUCE

This BBQ sauce, which has a kick thanks to the addition of chili powder, is great over potatoes of all kinds, tempeh, and tofu; in sandwiches and wraps; and even on pizza.

STUFF YOU NEED

1 cup ketchup

¼ cup white vinegar

⅓ cup brown sugar

3 tablespoons unsulphured molasses

3 tablespoons yellow mustard

1½ teaspoons onion powder

1 teaspoon freshly cracked
   black pepper

1 teaspoon paprika

1 teaspoon garlic powder

1 teaspoon chili powder

1 teaspoon salt

WHAT TO DO

1. Combine all ingredients in a medium pot and mix well.

2. Bring to a low boil over medium heat and simmer for 5 minutes, stirring constantly. The sauce will bubble and pop, so make sure you keep your heat on medium and stir constantly!

3. Let cool and serve. Store in an airtight container in the fridge for up to several months, or at room temperature for up to 1 month.

 # *cajun caesar* **DRESSING**

Caesar dressing is delicious, but unfortunately, it's full of tiny fishies. Anchovies are commonly found in most restaurant and store-bought versions. This recipe, however, is seafood-free and it's been upgraded to have a spicy Cajun twist.

STUFF YOU NEED

- ½ cup olive oil
- 5 tablespoons apple cider vinegar
- 2 tablespoons Dijon mustard
- 1 tablespoon unsulphured molasses
- 1 tablespoon soy sauce (or gluten-free soy sauce)
- 2 teaspoons fresh lemon juice
- 1 teaspoon Tabasco sauce
- 2 medium garlic cloves, peeled
- 3 tablespoons nutritional yeast
- 4 teaspoons vegan parmesan cheese crumble
- 1 teaspoon brown sugar
- 1 teaspoon freshly cracked black pepper

WHAT TO DO

1. Combine all ingredients in a blender or food processor and blend until completely smooth; usually 2–3 minutes on medium speed.

2. Store in an airtight container in the refrigerator for up to a month.

ginger cocktail **SAUCE**

This gingery twist on cocktail sauce is great for dipping vegan "seafriend" treats like the Hearts of Palm Nuggets (page 119).

STUFF YOU NEED

⅔   cup ketchup

2   tablespoons grated ginger

1   teaspoon apple cider vinegar

½   teaspoon fresh lemon juice

½   teaspoon Tabasco sauce

¼   teaspoon unsulphured molasses

WHAT TO DO

1. Combine all ingredients in a small bowl and stir until well-blended.

2. Store in an airtight container in the refrigerator for up to a month.

tangy tabasco DRESSING

Tabasco is pretty damn good on its own, but I wouldn't douse my salad in it. This recipe turns one of my favorite sauces into a dressing that tingles, but doesn't numb my tastebuds with heat.

STUFF YOU NEED

¼   cup olive oil

1½ teaspoons vegan mayo

1½ teaspoons apple cider vinegar

1   teaspoon Tabasco sauce

½   teaspoon maple syrup

½   teaspoon fresh lemon juice

½   teaspoon Dijon mustard

½   teaspoon dried basil

¼   teaspoon garlic powder

¼   teaspoon freshly cracked
    black pepper

½   teaspoon cane sugar

¼   teaspoon paprika

⅛   teaspoon salt, or to taste

WHAT TO DO

1. Whisk together all ingredients and store in an airtight container in the refrigerator. This dressing will thicken up as time passes, so I recommend consuming it within a few days.

TIP
If you love all things spicy, double the Tabasco.

cajun nacho SAUCE

This sauce kind of reminds me of getting nacho "cheese" from a gas station while on road trips. This may not be real cheese, but let's be honest—that gas station cheese wasn't real cheese either, and how much of that did you eat?

STUFF YOU NEED

½ cup plus 2 tablespoons raw cashews

¾ cup boiling water

2 tablespoons nutritional yeast

1 tablespoon fresh lemon juice

2 teaspoons Tabasco sauce

¾ teaspoon Krimsey's Cajun Seasoning (page 193)

¼ teaspoon salt

Pinch of cayenne pepper

Recommended topping: pickled jalapeños

WHAT TO DO

1. Place cashews in a heatproof container and pour boiling water over them. Cover and let sit for 30 minutes.

2. Transfer cashews and their soaking liquid to a blender or food processor. Add all remaining ingredients and blend for 2 minutes. It may seem like a long time, but this is the key to a smooth, creamy sauce. And it heats things up in the process so your nacho sauce will be warm and ready to pour.

3. Serve immediately! (Honestly, this sauce doesn't hold up super well—read my note below for more info). I love this sauce over potatoes, veggies, beans, and chips. Top with pickled jalapeños for an authentic road-trip experience.

TIP You'll want to store leftover sauce in the fridge, but be aware that over time, it will get thicker. If needed, just add a bit of hot water and re-blend for best consistency.

cali-cajun **SAUCE**

Makes 1 cup **GF**

This was the first sauce ever served at the North Hollywood restaurant. It was originally called "Krimsey's Sauce" and was much hotter, but those Cali nerds couldn't handle it...so I made them a toned-down West Coast version. And I guess I'm a Cali nerd now too, because I can barely handle the heat in this one these days.

STUFF YOU NEED

- 1   cup vegan mayo
- 1   tablespoon Tabasco sauce
- 1   tablespoon Crystal hot sauce
- 2   teaspoons freshly cracked black pepper
- 1   teaspoon garlic powder
- 1   teaspoon salt

WHAT TO DO

1. Whisk all ingredients together until smooth. Store in an airtight container in the fridge—it will last at least a couple of months.

cajun **RANCH**

The famous Cajun Ranch recipe...this was by far the most requested recipe from my restaurant, even long after we closed. After this book is released, will all of you still want to be my friends? (Sad face.) For an authentic restaurant taste, make sure you're using my signature Cajun seasoning.

STUFF YOU NEED

1   cup vegan mayo

2   tablespoons unsweetened non-dairy milk (rice milk recommended)

1   tablespoon Krimsey's Cajun Seasoning (page 193)

1½ teaspoons dried parsley

½   teaspoon garlic powder

½   teaspoon onion powder

¼   teaspoon freshly cracked black pepper

WHAT TO DO

1. Whisk all ingredients together until thoroughly blended. Store in an airtight container in the refrigerator. It will last for at least a couple of months.

buffalo cayenne **SAUCE**

This sauce was created as the restaurant grew, and our small subpopulation of spice extremists grew and began begging for a "fire alarm"–style sauce. Add extra cayenne pepper and/or white pepper if you are one of those extra-crazy people that enjoys losing feeling in your tongue after eating.

STUFF YOU NEED

1   cup vegan mayo

½   cup Crystal hot sauce

1½   teaspoons cayenne pepper

½   teaspoon salt

½   teaspoon white pepper

⅛   teaspoon liquid smoke

WHAT TO DO

1. Whisk all ingredients together and store in an airtight container in the fridge. This sauce should last a couple of months, no problem.

bourbon street SAUCE

Makes 1 cup GF

Although I visited New Orleans frequently as a kid, I (of course) always experienced a somewhat censored version of it. I remember peering nervously down Bourbon Street and wondering what went on back there... So naturally, I spent my eighteenth birthday there with friends debauching until the sun came up. The tangy and spicy flavor combos here remind me of what it was like to discover the wacky adult side of New Orleans for the first time.

STUFF YOU NEED

½ cup yellow mustard

½ cup vegan mayo

1½ teaspoons fresh lemon juice

1 teaspoon Tabasco sauce

1 teaspoon apple cider vinegar

1 teaspoon garlic powder

1 teaspoon freshly cracked
   black pepper

WHAT TO DO

1. Whisk all ingredients together until smooth. Store in an airtight container in the fridge—it will last at least a couple of months.

rémoulade **SAUCE**

In Louisiana, we just say "rémoulade" (no need for the "sauce" disclaimer). But in other parts of the US, "rémoulade" is a foreign word and needs a little more description. It's creamy, tangy, and just a tiny touch of spicy.

STUFF YOU NEED

1 cup vegan mayo

2 tablespoons Dijon mustard

1 tablespoon fresh lemon juice

1 tablespoon ketchup

1 tablespoon dried parsley

1 tablespoon Tabasco sauce

½ teaspoon unsulphured molasses

1 teaspoon garlic powder

1 teaspoon paprika

½ teaspoon cane sugar

¼ teaspoon salt

¼ teaspoon freshly cracked black pepper

⅛ teaspoon liquid smoke

Pinch of cayenne pepper

Optional: You may also add 1 green onion, very finely sliced, if you are going to use the sauce within a few days. Otherwise, omit because the green onions will go bad in a week or so. Note: That's 1 stalk, not 1 bunch!

WHAT TO DO

1. Mix all ingredients together until well blended. Store in an airtight container in the fridge. It will last for at least a couple of months.

smoked chili CHEEZE SAUCE

Makes about 1¼ cups **GF**

This sauce (pictured on page 170) reminds me of eighth grade, when I would attend my private school's high school basketball games. I'd order the nachos, but I'd get mine smothered in jalapeños, then sit back and hope that everyone would see my wall of jalapeños as a "do not disturb sign" in snack form and keep their distance. I was such a wallflower back then, and the nachos protected me from strangers.

Nachos were seemingly omnipresent in those places like refreshment stands where no-longer-kids, not-yet-adults got to exist without supervision for the first time. To this day, for a lot of people, nachos recall a weird nostalgic feeling of safety and comfort tied up with memories of our first tastes of freedom.

STUFF YOU NEED

½   cup plus 2 tablespoons raw cashews

½   cup boiling water

1   teaspoon olive oil

¼   cup chopped yellow onion

½   cup unsweetened non-dairy milk (rice milk recommended)

2   tablespoons nutritional yeast

½   teaspoon salt

½   teaspoon chili powder

¼   teaspoon garlic powder

⅛   teaspoon freshly cracked black pepper

⅛   teaspoon turmeric powder

6   drops liquid smoke

Recommended topping: fresh or pickled jalapeños

WHAT TO DO

1. Place cashews in a heatproof container. Pour boiling water over them, cover, and let sit for 30 minutes.

2. While the cashews are soaking, heat olive oil in a small skillet over medium heat. Add onion and cook, stirring once every 2 minutes or so, for 4–5 minutes, or until edges begin to turn golden brown. When finished, remove from the heat and set aside.

3. When cashews are done soaking, transfer them, along with their soaking liquid, to a blender or food processor. Add all remaining ingredients (including cooked onions) and blend until super smooth, about 2 minutes. It may seem like a long time, but this is the key to a smooth, creamy sauce. And it heats things up in the process so your sauce will be warm and ready to pour when it's done.

4. Serve with fresh or pickled jalapeños, if desired. Refrigerate in an airtight container for up to two weeks.

TIP Your sauce will thicken up when stored in the fridge, so if you'll be using it later, add a little extra non-dairy milk when you're ready to reheat it.

browned sage **BUTTER SAUCE**

This warm and buttery sauce is delicious on veggies, vegan meats (especially holiday roasts), and potatoes.

STUFF YOU NEED

½   cup vegan butter

½   cup unsweetened non-dairy milk
     (rice milk recommended)

1   teaspoon cornstarch

2   tablespoons chopped fresh sage

¼   teaspoon salt, or to taste

¼   teaspoon freshly cracked
     black pepper

WHAT TO DO

1. Melt butter in a small pot over medium-low heat. Add non-dairy milk and cornstarch and cook for 3–5 minutes, stirring constantly. Reduce heat slightly if the sauce begins to boil too aggressively.

2. After the sauce begins to thicken and brown, remove from the heat and stir in fresh sage, salt, and black pepper. Serve warm.

maple HUNNY BUTTER

Makes about 1½ cups **GF**

This sweet and fluffy whipped butter works well on cornbread, pancakes, toast, and probably anything else you could think of that could benefit from some sweetness. Growing up, we often ate homemade cinnamon toast for breakfast—this would have really made it extra special!

STUFF YOU NEED

1 cup vegan butter, softened at room temperature

¼ cup plus 2 tablespoons light agave syrup

¼ cup maple syrup

¼ teaspoon salt

WHAT TO DO

1. Whip all ingredients together with a handheld or stand mixer on medium speed for 2–3 minutes, or until thoroughly whipped. If you don't have a mixer, a spatula and human power works, too.

2. Store in an airtight container in the fridge. It will last several months.

semisweet chocolate DRIZZLE SAUCE

This sauce is meant to be more chocolate, less sweetness. Usually, I'm drizzling this over a dessert that is perfectly sweet as-is, so it doesn't need an extra sugar punch. If you prefer a more "chocolate syrup"-type sauce, double the sugar and add another tablespoon of water.

STUFF YOU NEED

1   cup water

⅔   cup unsweetened cocoa powder

¼   cup cane sugar

1   (10-ounce) bag vegan semisweet chocolate chips

WHAT TO DO

1. In a 2-quart pot, bring water, cocoa powder, and sugar to a boil over medium heat. Use a metal whisk to break up chunks.

2. Once boiling, remove from the heat and pour in chocolate chips.

3. Mix well with a spatula until chips are melted. Allow to cool.

4. Use immediately as a warm drizzle, or store in a sealed container at room temperature for up to a week. If you put it in the fridge, it will thicken significantly and will likely not be pourable, but it will last longer.

TIP If the sauce thickens up too much for your liking after storing, reheat by running hot water over the container. You may also add a little hot water to the sauce and stir to incorporate. Be careful with microwaving—the chocolate can easily burn.

simple homemade ICING GLAZE

This yummy icing recipe is meant for recipes like Cinnamon King Cake (page 221) and Scratch Sugar Cookies (page 241), but I dunno, maybe you want to put in on your pancakes or in your coffee, too. Live your life, my friend.

STUFF YOU NEED

1½ cups powdered sugar, leveled

2 tablespoons non-dairy milk or water (I use about 2¼ tablespoons of rice milk)

½ teaspoon vanilla extract*

½ teaspoon fresh lemon juice

Note: *For sugar cookies, I like to swap the vanilla extract for almond extract. It gives the cookies a lighter, sweeter smell and taste.

WHAT TO DO

1. Whisk all ingredients together, except 1 tablespoon of non-dairy milk or water. Add the last tablespoon of water or non-dairy milk slowly to achieve the desired consistency, plus extra as needed. (Less liquid will make a thicker icing, while more liquid will create a thinner icing.) Use immediately.

salted caramel SAUCE

Makes about ½ cup **GF**

I burned this recipe countless times before I finally got it right. The key is to stir continuously, be patient, and keep the heat low. The result will be an ooey-gooey caramel sauce that you won't believe you made yourself.

STUFF YOU NEED

- ½ cup cane sugar
- ¼ cup vegan butter, chopped into chunks
- ¼ cup unsweetened non-dairy milk (rice milk recommended)
- ½ teaspoon salt

WHAT TO DO

1. Heat sugar in a medium saucepan over medium-low heat. It will take 2–3 minutes before it starts melting, then you'll need to stir continuously for the next 5–10 minutes with a heat-resistant spatula.

2. The sugar is going to go through a few stages: white granular sugar, clumpy sugar, rock candy, applesauce, and then lumpy snot. When it gets to the lumpy snot stage, be on high alert. You'll want to add your chopped butter just as the last big chunks are melting.

3. Add the butter, and be careful. It's probably going to spit at you a bit, but you're not scared—you have a spatula to stir it and calm it down. Keep stirring until the heat gets the mixture back up to barely bubbling again, then give it one final stir and let it gently froth for 1 minute.

4. When the minute is up, remove from the heat and slowly add the non-dairy milk. Again, it's going to be an angry pan and try to spit at you. Just ignore and keep slowly adding the milk, stirring as you go.

5. Once the milk is mixed in, add the salt and keep stirring until the caramel cools down.

6. Use immediately as a warm drizzle, or store in a sealed container at room temperature for up to a week. If you put it in the fridge, it will thicken significantly and will likely not be pourable, but it will last longer. If the sauce thickens up too much for your liking after storing, reheat by running hot water over the container.

"Questionable Caramel"
SUPPORT GROUP SOLUTIONS

Did your caramel turn into a brick after it cooled? Next go-around, keep the heat low and move quickly.

Does your caramel taste like a burnt tire? Your heat was probably too high, and you may have let it bubble a bit too long.

Is your caramel grainy? Your sugar probably didn't melt all the way, so give it a little extra time (keeping the heat low) on your next try.

Dressing, Sauces, & Toppings   191

 *hunny* **MUSTARD**

I refuse to eat corn dogs without this sauce. It's kinda barely sweet, but mostly creamy and tangy. And it contains exactly zero percent bee juice.

STUFF YOU NEED

½ cup Dijon mustard

½ cup vegan mayo

2 tablespoons agave syrup

1 tablespoon fresh lemon juice

⅛ teaspoon cayenne pepper

WHAT TO DO

1. Mix all ingredients well to combine. Store in an airtight container in the refrigerator for up to 2 weeks.

krimsey's cajun SEASONING

Makes about ½ cup **GF**

This is my signature Cajun seasoning recipe; formerly used and sold at the restaurant in North Hollywood. I like to make my own Cajun seasoning because I can choose the highest-quality spices and tailor the salt content to my personal preference. Store-bought varieties often overdo the salt and skimp on (or even completely skip) the more expensive ingredients like white pepper.

STUFF YOU NEED

- 1 tablespoon white pepper
- 1 tablespoon paprika
- 1 tablespoon chili powder
- 2 teaspoons freshly cracked black pepper
- 2 teaspoons salt
- 1½ teaspoons garlic powder
- 1½ teaspoons onion powder

WHAT TO DO

1. Combine all ingredients in a small bowl and whisk until well-blended. Store in an airtight container at room temperature. Generally, you should replace spices every year, because they start to lose their potency. This recipe is no exception.

TIP If you're sensitive to spiciness, try cutting the black pepper and chili powder quantities in half. This is going to be used in your kitchen—make it how you like it!

garlic sourdough **CROUTONS**

I like to make a huge batch of these croutons and freeze the extras. Try tripling this recipe and see how long it lasts—I bet it won't be long. I recommend chopping the bread into 1-inch cubes, but really any size or shape works.

STUFF YOU NEED

4   cups diced sourdough bread
    (or gluten-free bread)

¼   cup olive oil

2   teaspoons minced garlic

½   teaspoon onion powder

¼   teaspoon coarse-ground salt
    (flakes recommended)

WHAT TO DO

1. Preheat the oven to 350°F and line a baking sheet with parchment paper.

2. In a large bowl, mix olive oil, garlic, onion powder, and salt. Throw in bread cubes and toss to coat.

3. Transfer cubes to the baking sheet and bake for 7 minutes. Then remove from the oven, flip the croutons, and bake for another 6–8 minutes, or until they are golden brown at the edges.

4. Allow to cool completely before transferring to an airtight container for storage. They'll keep for several weeks at room temperature, or just go ahead and play it safe by freezing them. They'll keep for months!

smoky maple BACON BITS

These mimic the savory, smoky flavor of bacon without involving any pigs (preferable, in my opinion). Just be sure you're buying coconut flakes—sometimes called coconut "chips"—because "shredded coconut" is something totally different and won't work well.

STUFF YOU NEED

2   teaspoons maple syrup

1½ teaspoons balsamic vinegar

1   teaspoon salt

1   teaspoon cane sugar

1   teaspoon vegetable oil

½   teaspoon liquid smoke

1   cup dried coconut flakes (not shreds), plus extra as needed

WHAT TO DO

1. Preheat oven to 375°F.

2. Mix all ingredients except the coconut flakes in a medium bowl, then add coconut flakes and stir well to coat completely. If you've got a little extra liquid at the bottom of your bowl after stirring well, add some more coconut flakes, 1 tablespoon at a time, to soak up the extra juice.

3. Transfer to a dry baking sheet and spread out coconut flakes evenly on the pan, doing your best to separate flakes as much as possible into a single layer. Try to keep them somewhat close, though, because rogue pieces off on their own will receive more heat from the pan and will be likely to burn.

4. Bake for 3½ minutes, then remove from the oven and stir.

5. Return to the oven and bake for 3–4 more minutes, or until they are medium brown (the color of pancake syrup) with some dark edges. Watch carefully, as they can go from perfectly well-done to totally burnt very quickly! Also be aware that the flakes will continue to brown and crisp for a minute or so after removing them from the oven, so you'll want to stir them one more time before letting them cool. Separate them so that they don't stick together as they cool down.

6. Once they're at room temperature, they'll crisp up! Use immediately, or freeze in an airtight container or bag and use as craved.

roasted & salted PECANS

Makes about 2 cups **GF**

This recipe can easily be adapted to make whatever quantity you need. If you like to make things in bulk, go ahead and make a whole bag and store the extras in an airtight container.

STUFF YOU NEED

2 cups raw pecan halves (about ½ pound)

Baking spray

⅛ teaspoon salt

WHAT TO DO

1. Preheat oven to 350°F.

2. Spread the pecans out evenly on a baking pan and spray lightly with baking spray. It doesn't take much—just 6–8 quick spritzes total. Stir halfway through spritzing to make sure you get all sides of the pecans. Note: If you do not have or do not wish to use baking spray, you can also lightly brush the pecans with vegetable oil or olive oil in a small bowl, stirring to distribute oil (but this is not recommended, as it's easy to over-oil them).

3. Sprinkle with salt and stir to coat.

4. Bake for about 12 minutes, or until pecans smell roasty and are just very slightly browned. Watch them carefully, because "very slightly browned" can quickly turn to scorched! Cool completely and store in an airtight container at room temperature.

candied **PECAN PIECES**

It was Antoine, a first-name-only slave gardener in New Orleans, who was the first to successfully propagate pecans. His discovery eventually led to the cultivation and popularity of the pecan throughout the world, as these decadent nuts were shipped globally from the Port of New Orleans. Enjoy these as a topping, or by the handful as a sweet treat. And don't forget to thank Antoine.

STUFF YOU NEED

½ cup cane sugar

1½ tablespoons vegan butter, melted

2 teaspoons unsulphured molasses

1 teaspoon water

¼ teaspoon salt

2 cups raw pecan halves

WHAT TO DO

1. Preheat oven to 350°F.

2. In a medium bowl, combine sugar, melted vegan butter, molasses, water, and salt. Mix well, then add pecan halves. Stir well to make sure everything is nicely coated.

3. Transfer to a parchment paper–lined baking sheet and bake for 12 minutes, stirring halfway through so they don't burn.

4. Allow pecan pieces to cool completely. The candy coating will harden as they cool off. After they have reached room temperature, you can use them as halves, or you can chop and crumble them into tiny pieces if your recipe calls for "crushed candied pecans." Store in an airtight container at room temperature for up to 2 months.

Cinnamon King Cake

Desserts

maw maw's **PIE CRUST**

This recipe was adapted from the pie crust recipe my Maw Maw used consistently over the years to bake perfectly flaky crusts. This works for both sweet and savory pies, and makes one crust. If you're making a pie that requires a top crust too, don't forget to double the recipe! The recipe is written so that you'll have a little extra scrap dough, because I hate stressing about making ends meet when I'm making a pie. The other bonus is that it allows me to make a little mini pie with my scraps, so I can taste test without having to take out a slice of my main pie.

STUFF YOU NEED

1½ cups all-purpose flour (leveled off, not packed), plus extra as needed

½ teaspoon salt

¼ teaspoon baking powder

½ cup vegan butter, chilled and chopped

¼ cup vegetable shortening

¼ cup cold water, plus extra as needed

WHAT TO DO

1. Whisk flour, salt, and baking powder together in a medium bowl.

2. Use a pastry cutter or fork to cut in chilled vegan butter and vegetable shortening until the dough looks like gravel. When you're done, there should be no pieces bigger than a pea.

3. Add water and knead until just combined. If it feels a bit sticky, add more flour a little at a time until it feels like Play-Doh. If it's a little dry, add a little more water, 1 tablespoon at a time, until it reaches a soft (but not sticky) state.

4. To use the dough immediately, flour a work surface and roll dough out to just about ⅛ inch thick, flouring your rolling pin as needed to keep things from sticking. Transfer to a 9-inch pie dish and cut extra edges off. Use a fork's prongs, your fingers, or the edge of a spoon to press into the crust edges to leave a symmetrical design. Refrigerate for at least 30 minutes before filling and baking.

5. To store, form dough into a ball (or split into two balls if you've made a double batch), wrap tightly in plastic wrap or store in an airtight container, and refrigerate for up to 24 hours or freeze it for up to 1 month. Defrost by moving to the fridge the day before it's needed, then leave out at room temperature for 1 hour before rolling.

TIP To easily transfer the dough from your countertop to the pie dish, gently roll the dough around your rolling pin, then use the rolling pin to move it and unroll the dough on top of your dish.

gluten-free PIE CRUST

Although I'm not a dedicated gluten-free baker, it did feel important to create a gluten-free pie crust recipe that works well and tastes delicious, because so many pie fillings are naturally wheat-free! Gluten-free dough does not act the same way as wheat-based pie dough, so we won't be rolling it out with a rolling pin—we'll be smooshing it into place. The main difference I notice in the final product is that the gluten-free crust is much crumblier and less flaky than its wheat-based cousin, but it's unique and delicious nonetheless.

STUFF YOU NEED

- ¾ cup white rice flour , plus extra as needed
- ½ cup potato starch
- ¼ cup cornstarch
- ¼ cup tapioca starch
- 2 tablespoons arrowroot powder
- 1 teaspoon xanthan gum
- ½ teaspoon salt
- ½ cup vegan butter, chilled
- 2 tablespoons vegetable shortening, room temperature
- 3 tablespoons cold water, plus extra as needed

WHAT TO DO

1. Whisk white rice flour, potato starch, cornstarch, tapioca starch, arrowroot powder, xanthan gum, and salt together in a medium bowl.

2. Use a pastry cutter or fork to cut in chilled vegan butter and vegetable shortening. When well combined, the dough should look like coarse gravel.

3. Add cold water and knead it with your hands until no loose flour remains. If it gets too sticky, add more rice flour, ¼ cup at a time until it feels like Play-Doh. If it's too dry and crumbly, add a little more water, ½ tablespoon at a time.

4. Flatten the dough ball slightly and transfer to your 9-inch pie dish. (Remember, we don't roll gluten-free dough with a rolling pin. We smoosh it into place by hand.) Use your fingers to spread dough out along the bottom and up the sides of the pie dish, watching out for thick spots in the bottom edges of the pan.

5. Continue spreading dough until there is even thickness across the bottom and up the sides. Allocate a little extra dough to the crust edges so that you have a thick palette to work with when pressing in edge designs later. If you have any extra dough scraps when you're finished pressing, layer them over the crust edges to create more volume.

6. Use a fork's prongs, your fingers, or the edge of a spoon to press into the crust edges to create a symmetrical design all the way around. Refrigerate the crust-lined pie dish while you make your filling and topping. (If you're making your crust ahead of time, wrap in plastic wrap or place in an airtight container and store in the fridge for up to 24 hours.)

7. Use immediately. If you're using a glass or ceramic pie dish, just make sure you allow the pie dish to come to room temp before placing it in the oven. (Otherwise, it could shatter due to rapid heat expansion.)

pecan walnut PIE CRUST

This pie crust has a nice nutty crunch and is great for no-bake recipes like Raspberry Mint No-Bake Cheese-cake Pie (page 215). This recipe also makes a fun base for ice cream scoops—just press it into a cookie-cutter shape and top with a scoop of your favorite flavor.

STUFF YOU NEED

1½ cups pecans

1   cup walnuts

3   tablespoons light brown sugar

3   tablespoons vegan butter, softened
     at room temperature

¼   teaspoon salt

WHAT TO DO

1. Pulse pecans and walnuts in a food processor until they're ground down, but not pulverized into dust. It should look sort of like fine gravel (not sand).

2. Add brown sugar, vegan butter, and salt and pulse again until everything is blended, stopping to scrape the sides with a spatula a few times during the process.

3. Transfer to a 9-inch pie dish and use your fingers to press the pie crust into about a ½-inch-thick layer along the bottom and up the sides of the pan.

4. To store, tightly wrap the pie dish in plastic wrap and store in the freezer until needed. Defrost 3–24 hours before using.

maple molasses **PECAN PIE**

Makes 1 (9-inch) pie **GF**

This pie has a sweet, crunchy top layer with soft, flavorful insides that still manage to hold themselves together. The rich tastes of molasses and maple syrup take this dessert from an ordinary classic to something extra-special, worth eating very, very slowly.

STUFF YOU NEED

- 1 pie crust dough ball (Maw Maw's Pie Crust, page 202, or Gluten-Free Pie Crust, page 203)
- ¾ cup packed light brown sugar
- ½ cup silken tofu*
- ⅓ cup vegan butter
- ¼ cup agave syrup
- 2 tablespoons maple syrup
- 1 tablespoon unsulphured molasses
- 1 teaspoon vanilla extract
- 2½ tablespoons cornstarch
- 2 tablespoons tapioca starch
- ½ teaspoon salt
- 1½ cups chopped raw pecans
- 1 cup raw pecan halves

For serving: vegan vanilla bean ice cream

Note: *Silken tofu is usually found in the Asian food section, not with the refrigerated tofu. It's very different from soft, medium, or firm tofu, and has a totally different flavor and texture. So no subbing here!

WHAT TO DO

1. Preheat the oven to 350°F.

2. On a lightly floured work surface, roll out your pie dough into a ⅛-inch-thick sheet. Lightly flour your rolling pin as you go to keep things from sticking. Transfer dough to a 9-inch pie dish and trim off excess edges. Press a fork or spoon into the crust edges to create a design. Place pie crust in the fridge while you prepare your filling.

3. In a food processor, puree the brown sugar, silken tofu, vegan butter, agave syrup, maple syrup, molasses, vanilla extract, cornstarch, tapioca starch, and salt. Blend until smooth, 30–60 seconds.

4. Remove pie crust from the fridge and add chopped pecans to the empty pie shell. Then pour the contents of the food processor over the pecans and spread to even out.

5. Cover the top of the pie with pecan halves in a circular pattern, starting at the outer edge. Keep the long sides of the pecans perpendicular to the crust, and make the pecans just barely touch each other when gently placing them (no need to smoosh them down). Work your way in towards the center in rings, then complete the final centerpiece in a flower or star pattern.

6. Cover with foil and bake for 30 minutes, then remove the foil and bake uncovered for about another 35 minutes, or until the crust begins to brown and the filling looks set (not too jiggly). By then, the top layer will have crusted over. The pie will still feel a little loose when you move it around, but it will set when cooled.

7. Let the pie cool completely before slicing and serving, hopefully with ice cream.

apple POCKET PIES

Makes 8–10 hand pies

These little handheld mini pies are great for gatherings, especially if there will be kids there. It's kind of like classic apple pie, but with more delicious flaky crust pieces to enjoy. The added spices also contribute some unique flavors that differentiate these pocket treats from traditional apple pie.

STUFF YOU NEED

- 2 tablespoons vegan butter, melted, plus extra for topping
- 1 teaspoon maple syrup
- ½ teaspoon unsulphured molasses
- ½ teaspoon fresh lemon juice
- 1 cup cane sugar
- 1 tablespoon all-purpose flour
- 1 teaspoon ground cinnamon
- ⅛ teaspoon ground nutmeg
- ¼ teaspoon salt
- 2 pie crust dough balls (Maw Maw's Pie Crust, page 202)
- 1¼ cups green apple, unpeeled and very finely diced into ⅓-inch cubes

Optional toppings: coarse sugar* and Simple Homemade Icing Glaze (page 190)

Note: *Coarse sugar has bigger grains than regular sugar and holds up to baking temperatures as a topping. If you don't want to deal with this, you can omit. But it's a nice touch!

WHAT TO DO

1. Preheat your oven to 350°F.

2. In a medium bowl, mix butter, maple syrup, molasses, lemon juice, sugar, flour, cinnamon, nutmeg, and salt.

3. Place your first dough ball on a floured work surface and roll it out into an ⅛-inch-thick sheet, flouring your rolling pin as you go to keep things from sticking.

4. Using a pastry wheel or sharp knife, cut a 6-inch-wide circle from the dough. Move the dough circle to a clean, floured area of your workspace and give it another quick roll-over with the rolling pin to flatten and expand it a bit. Don't forget to keep your rolling pin floured!

5. Place 2 tablespoons of diced apples plus 1 packed tablespoon of sugar mix directly in the middle of your dough circle. Be careful to keep the filling away from the edges, or they may not seal properly. Fold the circle in half and use a fork to press and seal the edges together (continuing to keep the filling away from the edges), then poke or slice the top 3–4 times to create steam vents. Use your pastry wheel or knife to clean up the sealed edges. Place on a baking sheet and set aside.

6. Continue cutting circles and adding filling to create the rest of your hand pies, whipping out the second dough ball when you run out of dough. When all the pies are completed, brush the tops with melted vegan butter and sprinkle a bit of coarse sugar on them.

7. Bake pocket pies for about 35 minutes, or until tops and edges begin to turn golden brown. To take these up a level, drizzle lightly with icing glaze after they've cooled completely. Tightly wrap or store in an airtight container at room temperature for up to 2 days, or in the freezer for up to a month.

brown sugar **SWEET POTATO PIE**

The confusion about the difference between yams and sweet potatoes will probably never be totally resolved. That's because these words mean different things to different people all over the world. There is no "correct" answer. Central Americans first cultivated sweet potatoes of many colors and varieties with thin, smooth skin and sweet, moist insides. Eventually, these sweet potatoes made their way north to be farmed by Native Americans. West Africans and Asians, on the other hand, grew what they called "nyami," which were similar to sweet potatoes but with thicker skins, starchier insides, and a more tubular shape. When African slaves saw these Central American sweet potatoes, they of course compared them to nyami, and that was eventually shortened to "yams." Since then, everyone has been confused. I'm going to call the orange ones "sweet potatoes," because that's what I grew up calling them, but you may also see them at the supermarket as "garnet yams."

STUFF YOU NEED

1   pie crust dough ball (Maw Maw's Pie Crust, page 202 or Gluten-Free Pie Crust, page 203)

2–3 medium sweet potatoes, skins removed (about 1½ pounds)

⅓   cup rice milk

1   teaspoon vanilla extract

5   drops anise extract

1   cup packed light brown sugar

¼   cup cornstarch

1   teaspoon ground cinnamon

½   teaspoon ground nutmeg

¼   teaspoon salt

Topping: vegan whipped cream, ground cinnamon

WHAT TO DO

1. Preheat oven to 350°F.

2. Prick sweet potatoes a few times with a fork and microwave until a fork easily pokes through to the center. This usually takes 6–8 minutes total, depending on the size of your potatoes. (You can also oven-bake them at 375°F for about an hour, if you prefer.)

3. Let cool. To speed up the cooling process, run cold water over the potatoes. When cool enough to handle, slice each one open lengthwise, scrape out the insides, and transfer to a bowl (discard skin). Mash the sweet potato pulp and measure out 4 cups sweet potato mash. Transfer to a food processor.

4. Add rice milk, vanilla extract, anise extract, brown sugar, cornstarch, cinnamon, nutmeg, and salt to your food processor. Blend until smooth, 2–3 minutes, stopping halfway through to scrape down the sides.

5. Pour filling into prepared 9-inch pie crust and smooth the sweet potato out with a spatula. Cover loosely with foil. Bake for 45 minutes, then remove foil and bake for about another 30 minutes, or until the top layer of the pie is set and turns dark orange and balloons up while the hot sweet potato lava ripples underneath. The crust edges should also be golden brown.

6. Cool completely for maximum firmness, then cut into slices. Serve with vegan whipped cream and a light sprinkle of cinnamon.

peaches 'n cream CUPCAKE PIES

Makes about 12 mini pies **GF**

Here's a semi-embarrassing fact about myself: I used to only eat hard peaches. As a teen, I enjoyed the apple-like crunch of biting into an unripe peach. Now that I'm older and appreciate the finer things in life, I wouldn't dream of purposefully eating an unripe peach, assuming I had a choice. You can use a regular pie crust for these cupcake pies, or the gluten-free option on page 203. Just remember that if you're going the gluten-free route, skip rolling out the dough since that doesn't work well. Instead, press the crusts straight into the cupcake tin using your fingers. Distribute evenly.

STUFF YOU NEED

Pie Cups and Peach Filling

- 1 pie crust dough ball (Maw Maw's Pie Crust, page 202 or Gluten-Free Pie Crust, page 203)
- ¼ cup all-purpose flour
- ¼ cup cane sugar
- 1 tablespoon cornstarch
- ½ teaspoon baking powder
- ¼ teaspoon salt
- 3 tablespoons vegan butter, melted
- 3 tablespoons unsweetened non-dairy milk (rice milk recommended)
- ½ teaspoon vanilla extract
- ¼ teaspoon almond extract
- 2½ cups diced fresh, peeled peaches (or 15-ounce can sliced peaches, well-drained)

Molasses Cream Cheese Topping

- ¾ cup powdered sugar
- ½ (8-ounce) package vegan cream cheese, softened at room temperature
- ½ teaspoon unsulphured molasses
- ½ teaspoon vanilla extract

Topping: ground cinnamon

WHAT TO DO

1. Preheat oven to 350°F.

2. Roll out your dough on a lightly floured work surface to ⅛ inch thick. Use a pastry roller or a knife to cut out twelve 4½-inch circles. Use your rolling pin to go over each circle with another pass and make them a bit larger and thinner. Transfer the dough circles to a 12-cup ungreased muffin pan, pressing the crusts into the bottom and up the sides of each muffin cup, then use any dough scraps to fill in any holes. Don't create a "lip" with the dough—just stretch it to the top edge and stop there. Place the pan in the fridge while you prepare your filling.

3. In a medium bowl, whisk together flour, sugar, cornstarch, baking powder, and salt. Add vegan butter, non-dairy milk, vanilla extract, and almond extract. Beat with a spatula until smooth, then fold in diced peaches.

4. Distribute filling evenly among pie crust cups.

5. Bake for about 50 minutes, or until the pie crust edges look golden. When the pies are done, they'll look a bit inflated and domed, but they will deflate and flatten as they cool (then you'll fill them with cream cheese topping).

6. While the mini pies are baking, blend all cream cheese topping ingredients together in a small bowl. Cover and refrigerate until ready to use.

7. Remove the mini pies from the oven and let cool to room temperature, then refrigerate for at least 1 hour to set. After chilling, add a dollop of molasses cream cheese topping to the depression in the center of each pie cupcake.

8. Finish with a light sprinkle of cinnamon and refrigerate until ready to eat. Cupcakes can be refrigerated for up to 1 week.

mississippi river BROWNIE PIE

Makes 1 (9-inch) pie

The original Mississippi Mud Cake is believed to have been named after the layers of mud along the banks of the Mississippi River. If you've been to the Mississippi River, that probably doesn't sound very appetizing, but I get what they were going for. My version is pretty sweet and really hits the spot when you're looking for something devilish.

STUFF YOU NEED

Brownie pie

1   cup all-purpose flour

⅔   cup cane sugar

½   cup unsweetened cocoa powder

4   teaspoons cornstarch

½   teaspoon baking powder

½   teaspoon salt

⅔   cup unsweetened rice milk

⅓   cup vegan butter, melted

Frosting

1½   cups powdered sugar

2   tablespoons unsweetened cocoa powder

¼   cup vegan butter, melted

2   tablespoons unsweetened non-dairy milk (drinking coconut milk, not canned, is recommended)

½   teaspoon vanilla extract

Toppings

1½   cups vegan mini marshmallows

⅓   cup mini vegan chocolate chips

⅓   cup Roasted & Salted Pecans (page 197), crushed

For serving: Vegan vanilla bean ice cream and Semisweet Chocolate Drizzle Sauce (page 189)

WHAT TO DO

1. Preheat the oven to 350°F.

2. Whisk together flour, sugar, cocoa powder, cornstarch, baking powder, and salt in a medium bowl.

3. Add rice milk and vegan butter, mix well, and transfer to an oiled 9-inch round pie dish. The batter will be thick and sticky, like buttercream frosting—use a spatula to spread batter out evenly over the bottom of the pan, and lift it up on the sides an inch or two as if you're making a crust. The batter will fall as it bakes, so don't be afraid to go high with it!

4. Bake for 30 minutes.

5. While the brownie pie layer is baking, prepare your frosting. Use a spatula to mix together all frosting ingredients in a medium bowl and set aside.

6. When brownie pie is done, remove from the oven and pile the marshmallows in the center of the pie. Line the outer inch or two with chocolate chips, then return to the oven for 15 minutes, or until the marshmallows are puffy and very lightly browned and the chocolate chips are melty but not liquidy.

7. Remove from the oven and let cool slightly, until the marshmallows shrink down. Microwave the frosting for about 10–20 seconds to make it easier to pour and spread, then spread frosting evenly over the top of the pie. Sprinkle crushed roasted pecans over the frosting.

8. Refrigerate for at least 1 hour until set, then slice and serve. If desired, drizzle chocolate sauce over each slice and serve with a scoop of ice cream.

coconut pineapple pecan CAKE

Serves 12–15

Also known as "Cajun Cake," this dessert was influenced by a mix of French and Southern cooking. It's kind of a twist on traditional fruitcake, only the Cajun version uses nuts instead of cherries, cran-berries, and so on, because these fruits were not readily available to Cajun cooks. Some variations of this use walnuts, but I prefer the Southern pecans.

STUFF YOU NEED

Cake

3   cups all-purpose flour (leveled off, not packed)

1½ cups cane sugar

1   teaspoon baking soda

1   teaspoon baking powder

1   (20-ounce) can crushed pineapple, with 100% juice

½   cup water

¼   cup vegetable oil

Icing

1   (13.5-ounce) can full-fat coconut milk

½   cup vegan butter

½   cup cane sugar

1   cup shredded coconut

1   cup chopped Roasted and Salted Pecans (page 197)

WHAT TO DO

1. Preheat the oven to 350°F.

2. Whisk together all dry cake ingredients, then add pineapple with juice, water, and oil.

3. Mix well and transfer to an oiled 9×13-inch baking dish.

4. Bake for 30 minutes, or until a toothpick comes out clean and the top of the cake is golden.

5. While cake is baking, make the icing. Combine coconut milk, vegan but-ter, and sugar in a saucepan over medium-high heat. Bring to a boil, then reduce the heat to medium and simmer for 3–4 minutes, or until the mix starts to thicken up.

6. Mix in coconut shreds and chopped pecans, then pour over the cake as soon as it comes out of the oven. Let cool before serving!

TIP This recipe can also be made into cup-cakes—just adjust the bak-ing time to about 20 minutes, or until tops are golden brown. Don't get the "lite" coconut milk! It makes everything watery.

raspberry mint no-bake CHEESECAKE PIE

Makes 1 (9-inch) pie; serves 6–12 **GF**

My mom used to pick fresh mint from our garden for our tea, so maybe that's why I grew up to love mint-flavored everything. In this recipe, the mint is almost undetectable, but it adds a little "tingle." You could make this cheesecake in a springform pan, tart pan, or even individual muffin cups. But I like everything to be pie, so I made this one a pie, too. It's technically "no-bake," but if you like the toasty flavor of roasted pecans and walnuts, pre-bake the crust for 10 minutes at 350°F, then put the pan in the freezer to cool down the crust before filling.

STUFF YOU NEED

1   Pecan Walnut Pie Crust (page 204)

Filling

1   (13.5-ounce) can unsweetened full-fat coconut milk, refrigerated in the can

16   ounces vegan cream cheese, softened at room temperature

1   cup plus 2 tablespoons cane sugar

3   tablespoons fresh lime juice

2   teaspoons almond extract

⅛   teaspoon peppermint extract

2   teaspoons arrowroot starch

2   teaspoons packed minced mint leaves

1   teaspoon salt

2   cups raspberries, divided

Toppings: Semisweet Chocolate Drizzle Sauce (page 189), vegan whipped cream, fresh raspberries, and fresh mint

WHAT TO DO

1. If you haven't already pressed your pecan walnut crust into your 9-inch pie dish, do that first. Try to make it about ½ inch thick and bring it up the side edges a bit.

2. Remove your can of coconut milk from the fridge and use a can opener to pop two holes in the bottom of the can. Drain out the liquids from the bottom, then open the can normally from the top. Scoop out the coconut milk solids and transfer to a blender.

3. Add cream cheese, sugar, lime juice, almond extract, peppermint extract, arrowroot starch, mint leaves, and salt to the blender. Puree until everything looks smooth, about 30 seconds, taking a break about every 10 seconds to scrape the sides with a spatula. Don't forget to scrape the underside of the lid, too.

4. Pour roughly a third of the cream cheese mixture into the pie crust and put the pie in the freezer. It's okay to guesstimate quantities—this part isn't scientific.

5. Add 1 cup of raspberries to the remaining cream cheese mixture in the blender and blend again for 30 seconds. Just like before, scrape the sides and lid a few times during the process.

(Recipe continues on next page)

(Recipe continued from previous page)

6. Check on your pie in the freezer. Is the top layer a bit firm? Firm enough to pour the next layer on top without them melting into each other? If yes, move on to the next step. If no, give it another 20 minutes. Patience is key with this recipe; it's how you're going to create those beautiful layers. Maybe have a cup of coffee or just sit and stare out the window quietly. (When was the last time you did that?)

7. Pour half of the raspberry cream into the pie on top of your first layer. Again, it's not science—just pour roughly half. Gently spread out the new layer and return the pie to the freezer. You'll probably want to wait at least 30 minutes before adding the next layer.

8. Add remaining 1 cup of raspberries to the cream in the blender. Blend and scrape until smooth, 30 seconds or so. When the second pie layer is set, pour this final layer on top.

9. Freeze for at least 2 hours, then move to the fridge to thaw a bit before serving. Top with whipped cream, fresh raspberries, and fresh mint. And don't forget the chocolate sauce! Enjoy all the compliments on your chef skills.

stuffed queen cake CUPCAKES

A sister to King Cake, these cupcakes resemble the cinnamon and nutmeg flavors of the Mardi Gras treat, but with a fluffier feel and bite-sized appeal. They're stuffed with Salted Caramel Sauce and topped with homemade buttercream icing. These cupcakes still work without the filling, so skip that if you're looking for something simpler.

STUFF YOU NEED

Cupcakes

- 2 cups all-purpose flour
- 1 cup cane sugar
- 2 tablespoons cornstarch
- 2 teaspoons baking powder
- ½ teaspoon salt
- ¼ teaspoon ground nutmeg
- ¼ teaspoon ground cinnamon
- 1½ cup unsweetened non-dairy milk (rice milk recommended)
- ¼ cup vegan butter, melted
- 1 teaspoon vanilla extract

Salted Caramel Filling (Optional)

Salted Caramel Sauce (page 191)

Buttercream Frosting

- 3 cups powdered sugar
- ¾ cup vegan butter, softened at room temperature
- ½ teaspoon vanilla extract

Recommended toppings: sprinkles and colored sugar

Special tool: For my cupcakes, I used a tricolor piping bag by Wilton. I love it! But even a Ziploc bag will work in a pinch if you're using a single-color icing. If you go the tricolor route, I recommend increasing the icing recipe volume by an extra 50 percent so you don't get stressed out about quantities.

WHAT TO DO

1. Preheat your oven to 350°F.

2. Whisk flour, sugar, cornstarch, baking powder, salt, nutmeg, and cinnamon together in a medium bowl.

3. Add non-dairy milk, melted butter, and vanilla extract. Mix with a spatula until combined and no lumps remain.

4. Line a 12-cup muffin pan with cupcake liners, or spray with nonstick baking spray.

5. Scoop batter into your muffin pan, filling the cups almost to the top (you only need to leave about ⅛ inch of room at the top).

6. Bake for 30–35 minutes, or until tops are lightly browned.

7. While cupcakes are baking, prepare salted caramel filling, if using.

8. To make the buttercream frosting, beat all ingredients together with an electric hand mixer, or use a sturdy spoon and some elbow grease. Set aside.

9. If using filling: Once the cupcakes have cooled completely, use a bread knife to cut a 1½-inch-deep inverted cone-shaped hole in the top of each cupcake, then use a spoon or piping bag to fill holes with salted caramel filling.

10. Transfer buttercream to a piping bag and pipe over the top of each cupcake, then sprinkle with colored sugar and/or sprinkles.

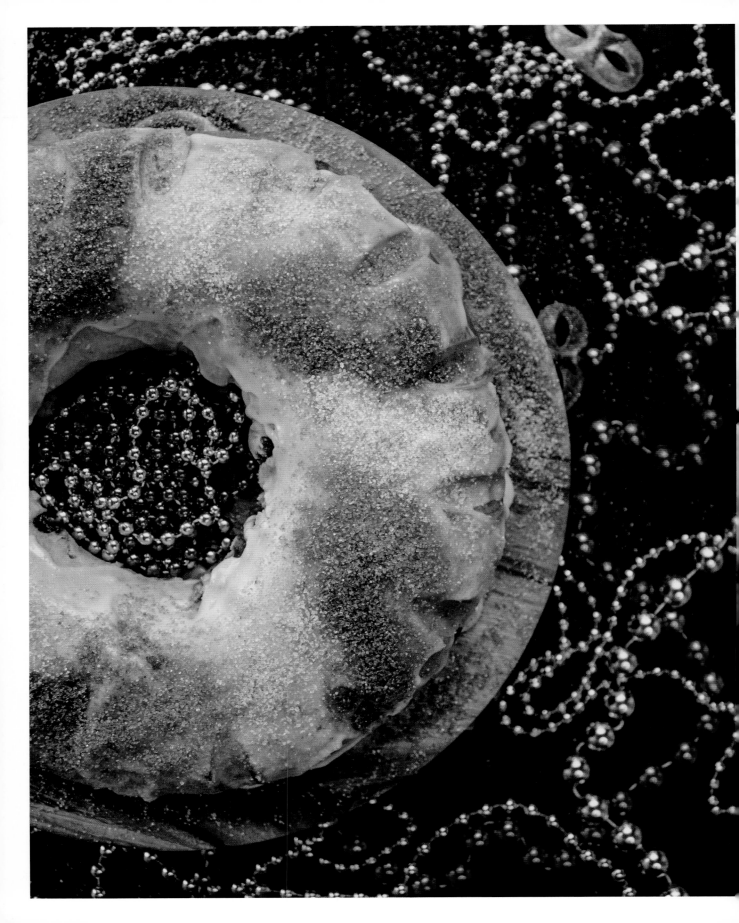

cinnamon **KING CAKE**

Traditionally, King Cake is supposed to be served beginning the twelfth day after Christmas up until Fat Tuesday (it's a Catholic tradition), but you'll sometimes see King Cakes popping up in Louisiana as soon as Thanksgiving. You're technically not supposed to bake it before or after Mardi Gras season, or else you'll bring bad luck and cause it to rain on Mardi Gras day. But we can't help it—we love our King Cakes.

Yes, this recipe looks long. That's just because I'm a stickler for good King Cake, and I did my best to make the instructions crystal clear. So don't be intimidated by the word count—this is a fun recipe, and you'll love sharing your delicious creation with friends and family when it's done!

STUFF YOU NEED

Dough

- 1⅔ cups unsweetened non-dairy milk (rice milk recommended), warmed, plus extra as needed
- ¾ cup vegan butter, melted
- 1 teaspoon vanilla extract
- ⅓ cup cane sugar
- 2¼ teaspoons instant active dry yeast (1 standard ¼-ounce packet)
- 1½ teaspoons baking powder
- 1 teaspoon salt
- ½ teaspoon ground cinnamon
- ½ teaspoon ground nutmeg
- 4¾ cups all-purpose flour (leveled off, not packed), plus extra as needed

Filling

- ⅓ cup vegan butter, melted
- 1½ cups packed light brown sugar
- 2 teaspoons ground cinnamon
- ½ teaspoon ground nutmeg
- ½ teaspoon salt

Icing

- 1 batch of Simple Homemade Icing Glaze (page 190)

Topping and Serving: Colored sugar (purple, green, and yellow) and plastic baby

WHAT TO DO

1. Combine non-dairy milk, vegan butter, and vanilla in a large bowl and whisk to mix. The temperature should feel almost too hot, but not so hot that it burns. Imagine a nice shower, and find that temperature for your non-dairy milk.

2. Mix in sugar, instant yeast, baking powder, salt, cinnamon, and nutmeg. Then begin adding flour 1 cup at a time, mixing as you go with a spatula. Once the mix becomes too thick to stir with a spatula, switch to kneading by hand. If the mix is sticky, add a bit more flour. If it's too dry, slowly add non-dairy milk to get it back to the right consistency.

3. Throw your dough back into the mixing bowl (make sure it's clean) and cover with a lightly dampened towel or plastic wrap. Leave to rise in a warm place for 1–2 hours, or until roughly doubled in size. Ideally, the temperature should be around 80°F—be careful not to put it somewhere too hot.

4. While the dough is rising, mix all your filling ingredients in a small bowl and set aside. If you're making your own colored sugar, I recommend doing that now, too. Wait on the icing, though. It can get a little crusty if you make it too early.

5. When the dough has finished rising, preheat the oven to 350°F.

6. Punch down the dough, then transfer to a clean, lightly floured surface. Roll your dough into a thick rope shape by hand, then use a rolling pin to flatten the dough out into a rectangle, about ⅓ inch thick. Don't be afraid

(Recipe continues on next page)

(Recipe continued from previous page)

to break out that ruler! I always do—it makes things easier and gives more consistent results. This recipe was written so you'd have a little extra dough to work with, so once you have your rectangle shape rolled out, cut off the extra edges and set aside. I recommend having a little fun with those extras by making some mini king cake rolls for taste testing.

7. Once you have your 9×22-inch dough sheet trimmed down, use your rolling pin to flatten out and taper one of the long edges. This will be the center of the cake, so we want that edge to be thinner. Start at about 3 inches from the edge, and roll and flatten gradually until the rectangle has stretched to about 11×22 inches.

8. Spread filling across the dough using a spatula, leaving 1 inch bare along the thicker long edge (opposite the side you just flattened). You'll need this part bare to seal edges together.

9. Starting with the thinner long edge, roll the dough sheet toward the naked-edged, thicker side. Use your fingers to pinch the edges together where they meet to seal.

10. Roll the dough log so that the seam side is down, then bring ends together to form a circle. Press the two ends together and pinch exposed edges to seal. Your cake should be about 10 inches across, for reference.

11. Place on a parchment paper–lined or lightly oiled pan. I highly recommend using parchment paper, because your cake will probably ooze out a little filling, and that can be a sticky mess to clean up. Slice some shallow cuts into the outer edges of the cake (optional—this is mostly aesthetic). Bake for about 40 minutes, or until the top of the cake is golden brown and the cake makes a hollow sound when tapped.

12. When the cake has cooled, inspect the bottom. Use a cheese grater or bread knife to scrape off any burnt filling or edges (it's okay, it happens—no biggie). If using a plastic baby, press the baby into the cooled cake from the bottom. Just be sure to warn everyone that their food contains a non-edible item!

13. Let cool completely before icing! I can't stress this enough. If you ice it while it's hot, your icing will thin out and be drippier than usual. Once the cake is completely cool, drizzle icing over the top and quickly throw colored sugar down before the icing loses its stickiness. You may use food dye (natural or otherwise) to create your own colored sugar toppings, or you can buy them premade.

14. Slice and serve. This cake can also be frozen to enjoy later! Just be sure to freeze it before icing and wrap tightly in plastic wrap or store in an airtight container. The cake stays good frozen for up to a week.

TIP This Cinnamon Sugar filling is my favorite, but I hope you'll experiment and try some other fillings after you've mastered this beginner recipe! Back home, people love flavors like cherry, cream cheese, lemon, apple, strawberry, blueberry, and more. The sky's the limit...

double chocolate hex BROWNIES

Serves 12–15

These brownies are the perfect balance of chewy, cakey, and fudgy. They hold together well, if you can wait for them to cool first...but I know that's a big ask. If you want to do something fun with the leftovers, save half of the pan and make some Black Magic Brownie Beignets later (page 229).

STUFF YOU NEED

1   cup all-purpose flour

1   cup cane sugar

½   cup packed light brown sugar

½   cup unsweetened cocoa powder

1   tablespoon cornstarch

1   teaspoon baking powder

½   teaspoon salt

½   teaspoon xanthan gum

1   cup unsweetened non-dairy milk (rice milk recommended)

½   cups vegan butter, melted

½   cup plus 2 tablespoons vegan chocolate chips, divided

Topping: powdered sugar

WHAT TO DO

1. Preheat the oven to 375°F. Line a 7×11-inch glass baking dish with parchment paper, leaving enough paper on the long sides of the pan so that you can use it to lift the brownies out when they're done. This will make it much easier to cut and remove them, rather than awkwardly trying to jam a butter knife in there to dig out your treats. That's right, I see you, knife- and spatula-jammers...hunched over the pan eating brownie corner crumbles straight out of the pan with your hands like Gollum chomping on a fresh-caught fish. That works too, but try the parchment paper method if you're bringing them to a party where you'll have to share.

2. Whisk flour, both sugars, cocoa powder, cornstarch, baking powder, salt, and xanthan gum together in a large bowl, breaking up any flour or sugar chunks as you go.

3. Add non-dairy milk and vegan butter and mix thoroughly. Don't worry about overmixing—it will just help activate the gluten and bind your brownie batter in the oven.

4. Fold in ½ cup of chocolate chips, then transfer the batter to the parchment-lined baking dish.

5. Use a spatula to smooth and spread out the batter so it rests evenly in the pan. Top with your remaining 2 tablespoons of vegan chocolate chips.

6. Bake for 30–35 minutes, or until top layer is set and outer edges begin to darken.

7. Remove from the oven and let cool before removing from the pan. Use your parchment paper handles to lift the entire slab of brownies out of the pan, then cut into squares. Transfer to a serving platter and top with a light dusting of powdered sugar

8. If you have leftovers, transfer to an airtight container and store at room temperature for up to 1 week. You can also tightly wrap and store in the freezer for up to 1 month.

coconut rocky road CLUSTERS

Makes about 2 dozen candies **GF**

When I was nine years old, my mom sent me to school with a lunch box full of peanut clusters to share with my class for Valentine's Day. Instead of sharing them, I slowly finished off the whole lunch box by myself (they're that good)...then returned the empty lunch box to my mother and told her all about how the class loved them. And yes, I did get sick that evening. Here's my personal take on a classic favorite.

STUFF YOU NEED

1   (10-ounce) bag vegan semisweet chocolate chips

1   tablespoon coconut oil

⅔   cup whole roasted and salted peanuts

⅔   cup whole roasted unsalted almonds

⅔   cup vegan mini marshmallows

1   tablespoon finely shredded coconut

¼   teaspoon salt

Topping: coarse-ground salt, finely shredded coconut

WHAT TO DO

1. Melt chocolate chips and coconut oil in a double boiler, or heat in the microwave for 1 minute, then remove and stir until everything is melted. If chips do not melt completely, you can pop them back in the microwave for 10 seconds at a time, stirring after each 10 seconds, until fully melted.

2. Add peanuts, almonds, marshmallows, coconut, and salt. Mix well, then keep stirring until the mixture thickens up just slightly.

3. Use a tablespoon to scoop the mixture and drop candies onto a piece of parchment paper. Sprinkle candies with coconut shreds and coarse salt.

4. Let cool. This will take an hour or two at room temperature, but you can stick them in an airtight container in the fridge if you just can't wait.

french quarter BEIGNETS

These beignets are light, fluffy, and come with a big pocket of hot steam in the middle. They're basically dessert pillows. I've eaten a lot of beignets over the years, and this recipe is an evolution of some of my favorites. Some places make "batter beignets," which are more like funnel cakes (where a liquid dough is dropped into the fryer), but this rolled and cut yeast dough is where it's at for me. If these are the first beignets you ever eat, you might be disappointed when you finally make it to the French Quarter and try those. These are the bomb.

STUFF YOU NEED

3   tablespoons vegan butter, melted

3   tablespoons cane sugar

1¼ teaspoons instant dry active yeast (about ½ a standard packet)

½   teaspoon salt

¼   teaspoon ground nutmeg

1¼ cups warm water, plus extra as needed

3½ cups all-purpose flour (leveled off, not packed), plus extra as needed

Frying oil (canola recommended)

Topping: powdered sugar

WHAT TO DO

1. In a large bowl, whisk together vegan butter, sugar, instant yeast, salt, nutmeg, and warm water. The water should feel hot, but not so hot that it burns. Imagine a nice shower and find that water temperature.

2. Add flour 1 cup at a time. Mix with a spoon or spatula until it's too difficult to stir, then switch to kneading with your hands.

3. Remove the dough from the bowl and knead on your countertop until just combined (don't overdo it). It should feel like soft Play-Doh that's just barely sticky. If the dough is too sticky to work with, add a little flour, just a tablespoon or two at a time. If it's too dry, add a little more warm water.

4. Wash and dry your large bowl, then grease with baking spray or a little bit of olive oil. Return the dough ball to the bowl and flip the dough around to cover all sides with a light oil coating.

5. Cover the bowl with a lightly dampened towel or plastic wrap. Let rise in a warm, but not hot, spot (about 80°F is perfect) until soft and roughly doubled in size, usually 1½–2 hours. It is important to let the dough rise properly, but not leave it sitting too long! If you must interrupt the rising process, the dough can be kept in the fridge for up to 24 hours, then returned to a warm spot to continue rising.

6. When your dough is almost ready, begin preheating your frying oil. If using a mini electric fryer, fill the fryer with oil and set the temperature to 375°F. To fry on the stovetop, review the important notes for success on page 21. For this recipe, you'll want to have at least 2 inches of oil in your frying pot.

(Recipe continues on next page)

(Recipe continued from previous page)

7. Once dough has doubled in size, place it on a lightly floured surface and punch it back down with your hands. Use a rolling pin to roll out to ⅛ inch thick. Work patiently so that the dough doesn't fight you too much. If the dough is too sticky, dust very lightly with flour. As you roll the dough out, flip it every now and then so the top surface is underneath, and vice versa. You'll notice that the dough probably wants to "shrink" after rolling out. That's okay, keep rolling and be patient until your dough sheet stabilizes at about ⅛ inch thick.

8. When you're ready to cut the dough, give it one more flip and then use a pastry wheel or sharp knife to cut into 3½x3½-inch squares, or whatever size suits you. I recommend cutting and frying a tester one first, then cutting the rest of the dough.

9. Use tongs to drop one beignet into hot fryer oil and cook for about 45 seconds on each side, or until light golden brown. It should puff up like a little pillow. When done, use tongs to remove from oil and place on a paper towel-lined to cool. Taste test. If there are some doughy sections in the middle, check to make sure your frying temperature is accurate. If it is accurate, increase your cook time slightly and use tongs to hold any raw corners under the oil to make sure they get cooked properly. If your beignet came out crunchy, check your temperature again and reduce cook time if needed. (Having other problems? Check out the support group solutions at right.)

10. Once your tester beignet has cooked to your liking, it's time to make the rest. Working in batches of 2–3, drop beignets into hot fryer oil and cook for about 45 seconds on each side, or until light golden brown.

11. When done, use tongs to remove from oil and place on a paper towel-lined plate to cool. Dust with powdered sugar and serve immediately. Watch out for hot steam when taking your first bite. I hope these take you straight to New Orleans, just like they do for me.

"Beignets for Days"
SUPPORT GROUP SOLUTIONS

If your beignets are coming out like pita chips, the dough is too thin.

If your beignets are coming out like dense bricks, your dough is too thick. The gluten is probably rebelling against all of the handling. Just let it sit for 10–20 minutes and come back to it—the dough should have relaxed a bit by then.

If your beignets won't puff up, try rolling the dough out a bit thinner and then letting the cut squares sit for a few minutes.

If you're getting holes in your dough, it could be a few things:
- It's rolled out way too thin.
- It needs a little extra flour (if it's sticky and it's getting holes, it probably needs more flour).
- You're trying to bully your dough into flattening out too quickly. Be gentle and work slowly.

black magic BROWNIE BEIGNETS

I don't believe in evil magic, spells, or demons. But I do believe in the magical, seductive powers of these brownie beignets. When making these, view it as an art project—it's gonna be a little messy, but it's going to be delicious, and it's going to be yours. You can stuff your beignets with anything you'd like—peaches, strawberries, cream cheese, cinnamon sugar, apples, vegan sausage, cookies, jambalaya, vegan cheese—so I hope you try out some other stuffings, too!

STUFF YOU NEED

1¼ cups warm water

3   tablespoons vegan butter, melted

3   tablespoons cane sugar

1¼ teaspoons instant dry active yeast
     (about ½ a standard packet)

½   teaspoon salt

¼   teaspoon ground nutmeg

3½ cups all-purpose flour

Frying oil (canola recommended)

½   batch prepared Double Chocolate
     Hex Brownies (page 223), cut
     into 2×2-inch squares

Topping: powdered sugar

WHAT TO DO

1. In a large bowl, whisk together warm water, vegan butter, sugar, yeast, salt, and nutmeg. The water should feel hot, but not so hot that it burns. Imagine a nice shower and find that water temperature.

2. Add flour 1 cup at a time. Mix with a spoon or spatula until it's too difficult to stir, then switch to kneading with your hands.

3. Remove the dough from the bowl and knead on your countertop until just combined (don't overdo it). It should feel like soft Play-Doh that's just barely sticky. If the dough is too sticky to work with, add a little flour a tablespoon or two at a time. If it's too dry, add a little more warm water.

4. Wash and dry your large bowl, then grease with baking spray or a little bit of olive oil. Return the dough ball to the bowl and flip the dough around to coat all sides lightly with oil.

5. Cover the bowl with a lightly dampened towel or plastic wrap. Let rise in a warm, but not hot, spot (about 80°F is perfect) until soft and roughly doubled in size, usually 1½–2 hours. It is important to let the dough rise properly, but not leave it sitting too long! If you must interrupt the rising process, the dough can be kept in the fridge for up to 24 hours, then return it to a warm spot to continue letting it rise.

6. When your dough is almost ready, begin preheating your frying oil. If using a mini electric fryer, fill the fryer with oil and set the temperature to 375°F. To fry on the stovetop, review the important notes for success on

(Recipe continues on next page)

(Recipe continued from previous page)

page 21. For this recipe, you'll want to have at least 2 inches of oil in your frying pot.

7. Once dough has doubled in size, place it on a lightly floured surface and punch it back down with your hands. Use a rolling pin to roll out a ⅛-inch-thick dough sheet. Work patiently so that the dough doesn't fight you too much. If the dough is too sticky, dust very lightly with flour. As you roll the dough out, flip it every now and then so the top surface is underneath, and vice versa. You'll notice that the dough probably wants to "shrink" after rolling out. That's okay, keep rolling and be patient until your dough sheet stabilizes at about ⅛ inch thick.

8. When you're ready to cut the dough, give it one more flip, then place a brownie square onto a corner of the dough. Cut out a 3×3-inch piece from another section of the dough, then place it on top of the brownie. Squish the edges of the top piece into the bottom piece, then squish the brownie around inside the pocket a bit to flatten it out. Use a scalloped pastry wheel or knife to cut a circle around the brownie along the sealed edges.

9. Use tongs to drop your beignet into the hot fryer oil, then cook for 45–60 seconds on each side, or until light golden brown.

10. When done, use tongs to remove from oil and place on a paper towel-lined plate to cool. Taste test. If there are some doughy sections in the middle, check to make sure your frying temperature is accurate. If it is accurate, increase your cook time slightly and use tongs to hold any raw corners under the oil to make sure they get cooked properly. If your beignet came out crunchy, check your temperature again and reduce cook time if needed. (Having other problems? Check out the support group solutions at right.)

11. Once your tester beignet has cooked to your liking, it's time to make the rest. Continue cutting, stuffing, and cooking your beignets in batches of 2–3 at a time.

12. Top with powdered sugar and serve immediately.

"Beignets for Days"
SUPPORT GROUP SOLUTIONS

If your beignets are coming out like pita chips, the dough is too thin.

If your beignets are coming out like dense bricks, your dough is too thick. The gluten is probably rebelling against all of the handling. Just let it sit for 10–20 minutes and come back to it—the dough should have relaxed a bit by then.

If your beignets won't puff up, try rolling the dough out a bit thinner and then letting the cut squares sit for a few minutes.

If you're getting holes in your dough, it could be a few things:

- It's rolled out way too thin.
- It needs a little extra flour (if it's sticky and it's getting holes, it probably needs more flour).
- You're trying to bully your dough into flattening out too quickly. Be gentle and work slowly.

salted pecan PRALINES

Pralines were originally a French almond candy, but since almonds were in short supply in Louisiana in the 1700s, cooks began making them with pecans. This recipe is an adaption of the classic pecan version; it's what most people think of when they think of Southern praline candies. If you want to sub in regular pecans instead of the Roasted & Salted Pecans, that will technically work. But the roasted pecans make these crazy over-the-top good with their light crunch and toasty flavor.

STUFF YOU NEED

2 cups cane sugar

⅔ cup non-dairy liquid coconut* coffee creamer

1 tablespoon unsulphured molasses

¼ cup vegan butter, chilled

1 teaspoon vanilla extract

¼ teaspoon salt

1½ cups Roasted & Salted Pecans (page 197)

Topping: coarse-ground salt

Special tools: 1/8 cup scoop or measuring cup and mini spatula

Note: *You may also sub in any non-dairy liquid coffee creamer, but the coconut creamer has a higher fat content and helps create a creamier taste and texture.

WHAT TO DO

1. Cover a flat surface (like your countertop) with a large sheet of parchment paper at least 24 inches long. You can also use a reusable silicone mat, if you have one.

2. In a 4-quart pot, heat sugar, coconut creamer, and molasses over medium heat. (I usually set my burner to a 6–7 out of 10 for this recipe.) Stir to mix, then allow the pot to heat up, but keep a close eye on it.

3. Once the sugar starts to bubble and froth up, cook for exactly 3 minutes, stirring occasionally, then remove from heat.

4. Add vegan butter, vanilla extract, and salt, then stir in pecans. Use a mini spatula to stir constantly until the candy mixture has cooled down slightly, 3–5 minutes.

5. Once the mixture starts to look a little thicker and less glossy, spoon a tester praline out onto the parchment. I like to use a ⅛-cup scoop, but a spoon works, too. I also recommend using a mini spatula to clean out your scoop after each praline. The praline mix should ooze outward slowly without being overly liquidy. Work as quickly as you can, because the mixture will begin solidifying within a few minutes. If it hardens up on you, just warm it back up briefly on the stovetop using the lowest setting possible.

6. If your tester went well, continue spooning out pralines until you've used up all the pecan mixture. If your tester was too liquidy, give it a little more time and keep stirring. If clumpy and hard, return the pot to the stove and warm for 30 seconds on low heat. Stir and try again.

7. When finished, grind some coarse salt over the top of each praline.

8. Allow to cool completely, then store in an airtight container with a parchment sheet between layers for up to 1 week.

caramel apple **BREAD PUDDING**

The origins of this dish date back over a thousand years ago to eleventh-century England. Back then, it was a "poor man's pudding"; a popular lower-class dish meant to make use of stale bread. Over time, bread pudding made its way around the world, but it has been particularly popular in the South. Ironically, we now sometimes leave bread out on purpose to make it stale for this dish. What a flip.

STUFF YOU NEED

1   (13.5-ounce) full-fat can of unsweetened coconut milk

½   cup unsweetened non-dairy milk (rice milk recommended)

2   tablespoons unsulphured molasses

2   teaspoons vanilla extract

1¼ cups cane sugar

1   tablespoon cornstarch

2   teaspoons ground cinnamon

1¼ teaspoons salt, divided

½   teaspoon ground nutmeg

1   stale* baguette (about 9 cups diced)

¼   cup vegan butter

4   cups diced apples, skin on (about 4 medium apples, any variety**)

½   cup packed light brown sugar

Recommended toppings: Salted Caramel Sauce (page 191), Candied Pecan Pieces (page 199), powdered sugar, non-dairy vanilla ice cream

Notes: *Stale bread is best, because it will be dry enough to soak up the delicious bread pudding liquids. **My favorite apples for bread pudding are Granny Smith (green), Fuji, and Honeycrisp apples. Try mixing them up together!

WHAT TO DO

1. Preheat the oven to 350°F.

2. In a large bowl, whisk together coconut milk, non-dairy milk, molasses, vanilla extract, sugar, cornstarch, cinnamon, 1 teaspoon of salt, and nutmeg.

3. Cut or tear bread into 1-inch cubes (some smaller cubes are okay, but no bigger) and add to the bowl. Toss to coat. Let sit while you prepare your apples.

4. In a 3-quart pot, melt vegan butter over medium heat. Add diced apples, light brown sugar, and remaining ¼ teaspoon salt. Cook for 5–6 minutes, stirring occasionally until apples are tender. Add half of the apple mixture to the bread bowl, and set the other half aside.

5. Transfer bread mixture to a greased or parchment-lined 9×13-inch baking dish. Use a spatula to flatten and even out the bread mixture. Top with the reserved apples, then bake for 40 minutes, or until nearly all of the liquid has been absorbed. The top should feel a bit crunchy, and the insides should be soft, but will firm up after cooling.

6. Let cool completely, then cut into slices, add your preferred toppings, and serve!

chocolate almond mint **MOUSSE**

Makes about 2½ cups **GF**

Let me be straight with you: Mousse is just fancy pudding. Or should I say, pudding for adults. And it's great for hot Southern summer days. The inspiration behind this recipe? Those delicious Andes dinner mints, which I first discovered at Piccadilly, a Baton Rouge–born Southern cafeteria-style restaurant chain (I loved their chocolate pies).

STUFF YOU NEED

1   (10-ounce) bag vegan semisweet chocolate chips

1   (12-ounce) package silken tofu*

⅔   cup powdered sugar

2   tablespoons cornstarch

2   tablespoons tapioca starch

1   tablespoon unsweetened non-dairy milk

1½ teaspoons almond extract

1½ teaspoons almond oil

½   teaspoon peppermint extract (or up to 1 teaspoon if you're a mint lover)

Recommended toppings: vegan whipped cream, chocolate shavings, vegan candies, almonds, and fresh mint leaves

Notes: *Silken tofu is usually found in the Asian food section, not with the refrigerated tofu. It's very different from soft, medium, or firm tofu, and has a totally different flavor and texture. So no subbing here!

WHAT TO DO

1. Melt chocolate chips in a double boiler, or heat in the microwave for 1 minute, then remove and stir until everything is melted. If chips do not melt completely, you can pop them back in the microwave for 10 seconds at a time, stirring after each 10 seconds, until fully melted.

2. Combine melted chocolate chips, silken tofu, powdered sugar, cornstarch, tapioca starch, non-dairy milk, almond extract, almond oil, and peppermint extract in a food processor. Blend until completely smooth, about 1 minute, stopping halfway through to scrape the sides with a spatula.

3. Refrigerate for at least 1 hour and serve chilled. If making ahead, it will keep for up to 1 week.

bananas FOSTER

Serves 3–4 **GF**

This is a pretty classic recipe that I didn't mess with too much, because it's just freakin' delicious. It was originally created by Chef Paul Blangé in 1951 to help promote the sale of bananas, which were imported through the Port of New Orleans. My version of his epic dish doesn't include rum, because I don't do booze at the moment and I don't think it adds much to the flavor appeal anyway. So traditionally, you'd light this dish on fire at the end (that's the reason for the rum)...but without the liquor, it's not very flammable. I'd say that's a positive (at least in my kitchen).

STUFF YOU NEED

½   cup packed light brown sugar

¼   cup maple syrup

2   teaspoons fresh lemon juice

1½ teaspoons vanilla extract

1½ teaspoons almond extract

1   teaspoon unsulphured molasses

¼   cup vegan butter

¼   cup chopped walnuts

¼   cup chopped pecans

3–4 bananas, peeled and sliced lengthwise, then chopped in half crosswise

½   teaspoon ground cinnamon

For serving: vegan vanilla bean ice cream

WHAT TO DO

1. In a small bowl, mix brown sugar, maple syrup, lemon juice, vanilla extract, almond extract, and molasses. Set aside.

2. Melt vegan butter in a cast-iron skillet (or a regular skillet, if that's what you've got) over medium heat. Normally, sugary dishes in a cast-iron pan are a no-no because they break down the non-stick seasoning layer. So, only attempt this in your cast-iron pan if it has a hearty layer of seasoning built up on it.

3. When butter is melted, add sugar mixture and stir continuously until boiling rapidly. Add walnuts and pecans, then banana slices. Spoon sauce over bananas and cook for 1–2 minutes, just long enough to heat the bananas through. Any longer and you may turn them to mush.

4. Remove from the heat and mix in the cinnamon. Serve immediately with a scoop of vanilla ice cream on each serving.

TIP If you have a mini cast-iron skillet, this would be a really cute dish to cook up as a single serving (just make a ¼ of the recipe size and only use one banana.) Then you can eat it straight out of the skillet. But who am I kidding? I eat it straight out of the regular-sized skillet too.

pumpkin gingerbread chocolate chunk COOKIES

Makes 15–20 cookies

These are fluffy little cookies, like soft gingersnaps with a chocolate-pumpkin twist. I love all holidays, and I especially love making fun recipes to bring to gatherings. These are perfect for that, so don't be shocked if you get asked for the recipe. I hope this one helps make your holidays warm and memorable.

STUFF YOU NEED

1½ cups all-purpose flour

¾ cup packed light brown sugar

1 teaspoon baking powder

1 teaspoon ground cinnamon

½ teaspoon salt

½ teaspoon ground nutmeg

½ teaspoon ground ginger

¼ teaspoon ground cloves

1 cup canned pumpkin puree

¼ cup maple syrup

¼ cup unsweetened non-dairy milk (rice milk recommended)

2 tablespoons vegan butter, melted

1 tablespoon unsulphured molasses

1 teaspoon vanilla extract

5 drops anise extract, optional

1 cup vegan chocolate chunks, plus extra for topping

Toppings: coarse salt and coarse sugar

WHAT TO DO

1. Preheat the oven to 350°F.

2. Whisk flour, brown sugar, baking powder, cinnamon, salt, nutmeg, ginger, and cloves together in a large bowl. Add pumpkin puree, maple syrup, non-dairy milk, vegan butter, molasses, vanilla extract, and anise extract, if using. Use a spatula to stir. Your batter will be very sticky—that's normal!

3. Fold in chocolate chunks.

4. Use a mini food scooper or spoon to drop cookie balls (approximately 2 tablespoons each) onto a greased or parchment-lined baking sheet. Drop a chocolate chunk or two on top of each cookie and smoosh into the surface gently.

5. Bake for 10 minutes, then remove from the oven and sprinkle with coarse salt and coarse sugar. Return to the oven and bake for 8 more minutes, or until the cookies are set and the bottoms are light golden brown.

6. Serve warm with a glass of almond milk, or let cool and store in an airtight container for up to 1 week.

scratch sugar COOKIES

My Maw Maw always made sugar cookies for Christmas, and decorating them was a family event. They looked terrible, thanks to us. But they were always delicious, because my Maw Maw knew what she was doing. This recipe is a tribute to her.

STUFF YOU NEED

1½ cups powdered sugar, leveled

½ teaspoon salt

1 cup vegan butter, softened at room temperature

¼ cup unsweetened non-dairy milk

1 teaspoon vanilla extract

½ teaspoon almond extract

2½ cups all-purpose flour, leveled

2 tablespoons cornstarch

1 teaspoon baking powder

Recommended toppings: Simple Home-made Icing Glaze (page 190), vegan sprinkles, colored sugar, and decorating icing for edging the cookies

WHAT TO DO

1. In a large bowl, whisk powdered sugar, salt, softened vegan butter, non-dairy milk, vanilla extract, and almond extract.

2. Add flour, cornstarch, and baking powder. Mix with a spatula until well combined. The dough will be sticky.

3. Cover and refrigerate for 1 hour to firm up the dough. (You can also refrigerate it overnight, if desired.)

4. When ready to bake, preheat the oven to 350°F.

5. Once chilled, split the dough into two sections to make it easier to handle. Place half of the dough on a floured surface and use a rolling pin to roll it out to ½ inch thick. Sprinkle with flour as needed to keep things from sticking.

6. Cut into shapes using cookie cutters, then place on a greased or parchment-lined cookie sheet, spacing cookies at least 1 inch apart. If making multiple trays, place prepared tray in the fridge while you roll out the second half of dough.

7. Bake 20–25 minutes, or until edges are light golden brown. Transfer to a cooling rack. Repeat to use up all the remaining dough.

8. While cookies are cooling, whisk together all ingredients for your Simple Homemade Icing Glaze until smooth.

9. Once cookies are completely cool, spread icing on top and add sprinkles or colored sugar, if using. If you want to make your cookies extra photogenic, line the edges of the cookies with decorating icing before spreading the glaze inside the lines. Let sit for 1–2 hours to allow icing to dry into a glaze before serving.

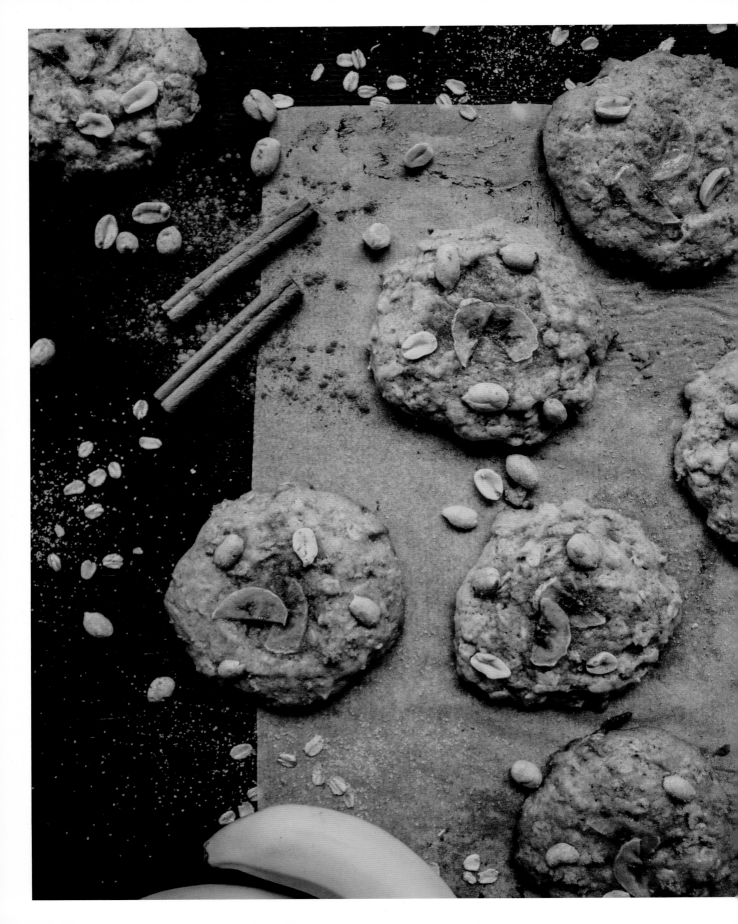

pb & banana **"MOOKIES"**

Like a muffin and a cookie had a baby...a delicious baby! Although bananas aren't grown much in Louisiana, the Port of New Orleans has historically been a major throughway for bananas coming in from South and Central America. So not surprisingly, bananas pop up in many Louisiana desserts. (Have you tried Bananas Foster? See page 239 for my version.)

Most peanuts in the United States are grown in the South, with Georgia being the majority leader. The far northeast corner of Louisiana also grows peanuts, because it has the right soil composition to yield a good crop.

STUFF YOU NEED

1 cup all-purpose flour

½ cup old-fashioned oats

½ cup cane sugar

1 teaspoon baking powder

1 teaspoon ground cinnamon

½ teaspoon salt

½ teaspoon ground nutmeg

½ cup mashed banana

¼ cup maple syrup

¼ cup natural, unsalted peanut butter

1 tablespoon vegetable oil

1 teaspoon vanilla extract

⅓ cup roasted and salted peanuts

Topping: banana slices, brown sugar, and roasted and salted peanuts

WHAT TO DO

1. Preheat the oven to 350°F.

2. In a large bowl, combine flour, oats, sugar, baking powder, cinnamon, salt, and nutmeg. Once blended, add mashed banana, maple syrup, peanut butter, vegetable oil, and vanilla extract. Mix with a spatula, then fold in peanuts.

3. The dough will be very sticky! Use a mini food scooper to drop balls of dough onto a parchment-lined or greased baking sheet, or just have fun with it and dig in with your hands! For large cookies, use ¼ cup dough per cookie; for smaller "drop" cookies, use 1 tablespoon.

4. Flatten cookies slightly using a spoon, and shape into circles—the cookies don't change shape much in the oven, so however you put them in will be roughly how they come out. Top each cookie with a couple pieces of thinly sliced banana, a sprinkle of brown sugar, and a few peanut halves.

5. Bake for 15 minutes for larger cookies, or until edges begin to turn golden brown. If you're baking smaller cookies, you will need to take them out a little bit early, so watch them. Allow to cool completely on the pan before serving.

fig & sweet potato oatmeal **COOKIES**

These are really something special when served warm with a cold glass of almond milk. They have just the right amount of sweetness, without being overly rich. Sweet potatoes, figs, and pecans make this somewhat of a Louisiana trifecta cookie.

STUFF YOU NEED

1   medium sweet potato

1¾ cups all-purpose flour

1½ teaspoons baking powder

½   teaspoon salt

½   teaspoon ground cinnamon

¼   teaspoon ground nutmeg

1   cup packed light brown sugar

½   cup vegan butter, melted

1½ tablespoons maple syrup

1   teaspoon vanilla extract

1   cup old-fashioned rolled oats

¾   cup diced dried purple figs

Toppings: pecan halves, brown sugar, and coarse-ground salt

WHAT TO DO

1. Wash and scrub your sweet potato, and prick a few times with a fork to allow steam to escape. Cook in the oven at 350°F for 50–60 minutes, or make it easy on yourself and microwave for 5–6 minutes instead, turning over once in the middle of cooking. Either way, cook until a fork can pierce through the center with ease. When cool enough to handle, slice open, scoop out the flesh, and mash. Measure out ½ cup mashed sweet potato and set aside. The rest of the potato won't be needed for this recipe, so do what you want with it.

2. In a medium bowl, whisk together flour, baking powder, salt, cinnamon, and nutmeg until well blended. Set aside.

3. In a smaller bowl, combine brown sugar, melted vegan butter, maple syrup, vanilla extract, and the ½ cup cooked and smashed sweet potato. Whisk together for 1–2 minutes, or until no large sweet potato chunks remain. Small ones are fine!

4. Slowly add sweet potato mixture to the dry ingredients, and stir with a spatula until combined. Fold in oats and figs.

5. Place cookie dough in the fridge and let chill for 20 minutes—this will get rid of the stickiness and make it easier to work with the dough. Meanwhile, preheat the oven to 350°F.

6. When dough has cooled, shape into 2-inch balls, then flatten into round cookie shapes on a lightly oiled or parchment-lined cookie sheet, about 1 inch apart. Press 2–3 pecan halves into the top of each cookie, then sprinkle with brown sugar and coarse-ground salt. Bake for 18–20 minutes, or until cookies are set and bottoms are golden brown.

7. Allow to cool on the pan for at least 20 minutes so that the cookies can set. Store in an airtight container for up to 1 week.

Hurricane Party

Drinks

southern **SWEET TEA**

My mom used to pick fresh mint from the garden to flavor our homemade tea, and it's a tradition that I still enjoy carrying on myself. When it comes to sweet tea, there's no "right way" to make it. It's just all about the tea-to-sugar ratio you prefer. Personally, I'm an unsweetened tea kinda gal, but I do enjoy the occasional step back in time with a glass of ice-cold Southern Sweet Tea.

STUFF YOU NEED

16 cups filtered water, divided

1 iced tea bag (made for a gallon of iced tea)

1 cup organic cane sugar

Fresh mint and lemon slices, for garnish

WHAT TO DO

1. Boil 8 cups of water in a 4-quart pot, then remove from the heat and add the tea bag. Allow tea to steep for 5 minutes—any longer than that, and your tea may start to get bitter.

2. Remove tea bag from the water, then stir in sugar while the tea is still hot to help the sugar dissolve. Transfer to a pitcher and add remaining 8 cups of filtered water. If you're a mint lover (like me), toss a couple sprigs of mint into your tea pitcher and let it diffuse.

3. Refrigerate until cold, then serve over ice with fresh mint and a slice of lemon.

"Spilling the Tea"
SUPPORT GROUP SOLUTIONS

The ingredients are important, yes, but it's more about how you do it. Here are some tips:

• Never boil a tea bag in the water.

• Choose tea bags that are made for iced tea. The only real difference between hot tea and cold tea bags is that the manufacturer measures the exact amount of tea needed for your (larger) specific volume. We used Lipton to make our signature sweet tea at the restaurant, but many Southerners also swear by Red Diamond. They're pretty similar.

• I don't do this (just to be clear), but there are people who suggest adding a little baking soda to your tea after steeping to keep it from getting cloudy and bitter in the fridge. They swear by it, but I guess I'm a minimalist.

country **LEMONADE**

This is a classic recipe that's a perfect balance of sweet and sour. I like to play with different variations, so if you're feeling adventurous, try making a glass of Jalapeño Cauldron Lemonade (page 255) once you've had your fill of the traditional version.

STUFF YOU NEED

1¼ cups cane sugar

4½ cups cold filtered water, divided, plus extra as needed

1¼ cups fresh lemon juice (from 5–8 medium lemons)

Lemon slices, for garnish

WHAT TO DO

1. Combine sugar and 1 cup of water in a medium pot over medium heat. Stir and heat until sugar has completely dissolved, 3–5 minutes. Let cool.

2. Transfer to a pitcher and add fresh lemon juice and remaining 3½ cups of water.

3. Taste test. I like my lemonade a bit intense, so if that's not your vibe, just add another cup or two of water. Keep in mind that serving it over ice will naturally dilute it a bit.

4. Pour over ice and serve with a fresh lemon slice.

This recipe is one of the simplest, but you do need to have Southern Sweet Tea and Country Lemonade on hand. I recommend mixing them fresh!

STUFF YOU NEED

1   part Country Lemonade (page 250)

1   part Southern Sweet Tea (page 249)

    Lemon slices, for garnish

WHAT TO DO

1. Pour equal parts Country Lemonade and Southern Sweet Tea over ice and garnish with a slice of lemon. Yes, it's really that simple.

ponchatoula strawberry **LEMONADE**

Makes ½ gallon **GF**

Every spring, Louisianans go crazy for strawberries. During peak fruiting season in April, the Louisiana town of Ponchatoula throws a huge party: The Ponchatoula Strawberry Festival, complete with rides, live music, parades, and strawberry-eating contests. The spirit of Ponchatoula is infused in this special strawberry lemonade.

STUFF YOU NEED

1½ cups diced hulled strawberries

1   cup cane sugar

4   cups filtered water, divided, plus extra as needed

1¼ cups fresh-squeezed lemon juice (from 5–8 medium lemons)

Lemon slices and strawberries, for garnish

WHAT TO DO

1. First, make your strawberry syrup. Combine strawberries, sugar, and ½ cup water in a medium pot over medium-low heat. Cook at a low simmer, stirring periodically to avoid sticking, for approximately 30 minutes, or until strawberries are fully broken down into a mush. Check on it frequently during the last 5–10 minutes of cooking.

2. Allow strawberries to cool, then transfer to a blender or food processor. Blend until smooth, 1–2 minutes. Be careful with hot stuff and blenders... things do explode.

3. Transfer strawberry syrup to a pitcher and add fresh lemon juice and remaining 3½ cups of cold water. Mix well. If the flavor is too intense for you, just add another cup or two of water, but don't forget that the ice in the cups will naturally dilute the lemonade a bit.

4. Serve over ice with a fresh slice of lemon and fresh strawberry.

TIP
Check out the recipe for Strawberry Shortcake Punch (page 259) if you want to make use of any leftovers!

lavender LEMONADE

When you've had as much lemonade as I've had, you start to look for ways to punch it up a bit. This lavender version is one of my favorites, and it's simple. I don't use a ton of lavender in cooking, so it's a nice break from my normal set of spices and flavors. Also, it will make you look fancy if you bring it to a party.

STUFF YOU NEED

1¼ cups cane sugar

4½ cups cold filtered water, divided, plus extra as needed

2 teaspoons dried culinary lavender (or 2 tablespoons packed fresh lavender)

1¼ cups fresh lemon juice (from 5–8 medium lemons)

Lemon slices and fresh lavender sprigs, for garnish

Special tools: sieve or cheesecloth

WHAT TO DO

1. Combine sugar and 1 cup of water in a medium pot over medium heat. Stir and heat until sugar has completely dissolved, 3–5 minutes. Remove from the heat and stir in the lavender. Let sit for 30–45 minutes, then pour through a sieve or cheesecloth into a pitcher to strain out lavender.

2. Add fresh lemon juice and remaining 3½ cups of water.

3. Taste test and add another cup or two of water if you like a less intense lemonade. Keep in mind that serving it over ice will naturally dilute it a bit.

4. Pour over ice and serve with a fresh lemon slice and sprig of lavender.

jalapeño cauldron LEMONADE

I originally created this recipe as a joke, but let me tell you—it's no joke! We started serving it at the restaurant as a Halloween special, and it was a hit. It's not too spicy, just a little "tingly," and it's fun to watch the charcoal slowly creep down into the lemonade like black-magic smoke.

STUFF YOU NEED

1   jalapeño, sliced

8   ounces prepared Country Lemonade (page 250)

⅛   teaspoon activated charcoal
    Lemon slice, for garnish

WHAT TO DO

1. Slice jalapeño into ¼-inch-thick slices, then place 4 slices at the bottom of a 12-ounce glass or Mason jar and fill with ice to the rim.

2. Fill glass with lemonade to the top, then add charcoal. Careful...charcoal is messy.

3. Poke a toothpick through one or two of the remaining jalapeño slices (from edge to edge, not straight through the middle) and gently poke around your beverage to disturb charcoal. You should get a nice "witchy" effect from this as the charcoal begins to settle.

4. Add a lemon slice for garnish and enjoy the buzzy flavor of this fun drink.

*café* **AU LAIT**

In French, café au lait simply means "coffee with milk." It goes great with French Quarter Beignets (page 227) and Cinnamon King Cake (page 221). You can use any non-dairy milk for this one, but I always recommend coconut since it has a higher fat content and will feel creamier. As you can see below, the recipe is quite simple. On occasion, I like to add a pinch of cayenne pepper just for kicks.

STUFF YOU NEED

1 part coconut milk (sweetened drinking milk, not canned)

1 part hot coffee (dark chicory roast recommended)

Pinch of cayenne pepper, optional

WHAT TO DO

1. Heat coconut milk in a saucepan over medium heat until hot, steamy, and almost boiling.

2. Pour hot coffee into your mug and top with hot steamed coconut milk. Sprinkle in a tiny bit of cayenne pepper, if using, and stir well. Serve immediately.

strawberry shortcake PUNCH

This is a playful variation of strawberry lemonade that some of our restaurant employees used to make while at work. Eventually, we made it official and put it on the menu with some fun extra tweaks.

STUFF YOU NEED

1   Twizzler or Red Vine

4   ounces prepared Ponchatoula Strawberry Lemonade (page 252)

4   ounces coconut milk (sweetened drinking milk, not canned)

Fresh strawberries and vegan marshmallows, for garnish

WHAT TO DO

1. Cut the very ends off your red licorice to make a candy straw. Set aside.

2. Fill a 12-ounce glass with ice, then pour in strawberry lemonade.

3. Top with coconut milk and garnish with half a strawberry, vegan marshmallows, and the licorice straw.

hot chocolate MIX

Hot chocolate mixes tend to be gross and full of weird crap, so I like to make my own. Having a mix on hand also makes it easy to whip up a quick single cup when cravings hit.

STUFF YOU NEED

2   cups soy milk powder

¾   cup cane sugar

¾   cup unsweetened cocoa powder

2   tablespoons cornstarch

For serving: boiling water and mini vegan marshmallows

WHAT TO DO

1. In a medium bowl, whisk together all ingredients. Be sure to break up any chunks, and use a spatula to turn over the ingredients on the bottom of the bowl to make sure they are well mixed. I recommend pouring this through a fine-mesh sieve to find and break up chunks.

2. Store at room temperature in an airtight container for up to 6 months.

To make a single serving of hot cocoa:

1. Place ¼ cup mix in the bottom of a 12-ounce coffee mug.

2. Add ¼ cup boiling hot water and use a spoon to mix well. Once the mix has dissolved and all chunks have been broken up, add more hot water to fill the mug to ½ inch from the top. Mix again.

3. Top with mini vegan marshmallows and serve!

hurricane PARTY

I was attending my first week of classes at Louisiana State University when Hurricane Katrina hit in 2005 and shook Louisiana down. Hurricanes are a destructive force of nature that are not to be messed with, but they can also bring people together. We huddled together to watch the news on rabbit-ear-and-tinfoil antennas, drank too much vodka (and Everclear, regrettably), belly laughed, and periodically ran outside barefoot in the sideways wind and rain to experience Mother Nature's raw power. This personal twist on a Nola classic drink—the Hurricane—brings that playful and curious energy right back. (Picture on page 246)

STUFF YOU NEED

2   cups passion fruit juice

1   cup pure pineapple juice*

½   cup maraschino cherry juice (from a jar of maraschino cherries)

¼   cup fresh lime juice

Orange slices, maraschino cherries**, and mint sprigs, for garnish

Notes: *Pure passion fruit juice can be really tough to find. Usually, it's mixed with something like pear juice or grape juice—that totally works. Just try to avoid "juice cocktails" that are really just sugar-water with some artificial passion fruit flavoring.**When shopping for maraschino cherries, steer clear of artificially colored cherries (the super-bright-red ones) and opt for a jar without red No. 40, if you can help it.

WHAT TO DO

1. Whisk all ingredients together in a pitcher. Serve over ice, and garnish with orange slices, maraschino cherries, and mint. If you want to add alcohol, try rum. Best enjoyed in the company of people that make you ugly laugh.

fresh tomato BLOODY MARY

Fresh tomato juice is so crazy good! It's different from canned juice, which is cooked down before packaging. You can sub in bottled tomato juice, but it usually has additives and salt, so you'll need to cut back some of the other ingredients a bit to account for that (just taste as you go). If the thought of drinking raw tomato juice makes you gag, you could also simmer your tomato juice for about 10 minutes to give it a more traditional Bloody Mary taste. Still delicious, and still so much better than canned juice.

STUFF YOU NEED

4–6 pounds vine tomatoes, or your favorite tomato variety

2 large garlic cloves

3 tablespoons apple cider vinegar

2 teaspoons brown sugar

1 teaspoon vegan Worcestershire sauce, optional

1 teaspoon hot sauce (Tabasco recommended)

1 teaspoon unsulphured molasses

1 teaspoon prepared horseradish

1 teaspoon freshly cracked black pepper

½ teaspoon salt, or to taste, plus more for rimming glasses

¼ teaspoon celery salt

¼ teaspoon paprika

1 drop liquid smoke (literally, one drop—don't overdo it)

Pinch of cayenne pepper

Recommended garnishes: pickled okra, cherry tomatoes, celery, vegan shrimp, lemon, lime, olives, banana peppers, asparagus, pickles, mini sweet peppers, cucumber, jalapeño, pickled carrots, baby corn

Special tool: juicer

WHAT TO DO

1. Juice your tomatoes and garlic cloves. Juice enough tomatoes to yield 4 cups fresh tomato juice. Transfer to a pitcher. With a juicer, you can just throw the whole garlic cloves in, skin on. If you don't have a juicer, you can puree the tomatoes and garlic in a food processor or blender, then pour the puree through some cheesecloth or a fine-mesh sieve to strain out the pulp. You'll want to peel the garlic first in this case, though.

2. Add all remaining ingredients to tomato juice and refrigerate at least 1 hour.

3. When ready to serve, wet the rims of your serving glasses and dip in salt. Then pour in Bloody Mary mix and garnish your drinks in a way that feels ridiculous. The crazier it looks, the better it tastes (it's science). If you want to add alcohol, try vodka.

Restaurant Tribute

This cookbook wouldn't have been possible without my "Krewe"—the team of staff members that made my restaurant, Krimsey's Cajun Kitchen (2017–2020), possible.

Our Krewe was the lifeblood of the place. Without that specific group of people, the restaurant would have felt just a little bit blander, a bit less special. We celebrated those who came and went (as young restaurant staff tend to do), while many others stuck around for the long haul. Those were the ones who helped shape and mold the place over the years, and I became very proud of and weirdly protective of them. But even those who just passed through for a season were always a part of our family, even if for a short time.

Here are some of my favorite memories with the Krewe at Krimsey's Cajun Kitchen:

• Painting and decorating our original restaurant space with my friends and family. My sister, Jess, and I hand-painted a big Louisiana mural in the back of the space, and I loved coming in every day and being reminded of how much fun we had designing the space.

• Moving into our new and bigger corner space with the help of the Krewe. Everyone joined in, and we had such a fun time moving everything over and goofing around! Sure, we weren't 100 percent efficient, but we had a great time.

• Hosting "Make Your Own Succulent Garden" night! It was a mess. Who thought bringing dirt and plants into a restaurant was a good idea? Turns out, it was an incredible idea.

• Partying with our Krewe at our annual holiday parties, always held at my house. They were the best, even though I always stayed up way past my normal, boring 10 p.m. bedtime.

• Throwing our final Mardi Gras party in 2020. Every year, the parties got bigger and bigger. This year, we didn't know it was going to be our last, but we still partied like it was. I'm so thankful to have had this one chance to see all of our lovely guests and friends one last time—it would be only another month before COVID-19 hit and changed our plans in ways we could never have expected.

Acknowledgments

Scott, the tall guy from Tinder who offered me his stick-shift Nissan Versa hatchback after our second date so I could transport my giant cast-iron jambalaya cauldron to my first Vegan Street Fair. You have been here since day one. And when I knew I wanted to close the restaurant but couldn't quit, it was you who gave me the courage to actually let go and move on. You love me without strings or agendas, and you're probably the only person I know who doesn't get road rage. I hope we keep liking each other for a long time because being your roommate and partner in life is so freakin' fun.

Jess, my original and longest-standing friend. Thank you for taking every idea that I've had and making it much better than I was originally thinking. Holy cow, I can't believe you designed my original self-published cookbook from scratch on your own, and we actually managed to get that sucker printed! This version definitely wouldn't exist without you and all the work that you put in on version 1.0. I'm lucky that you're my sister. And thank you for always testing the red beans, étouffée, and cornbread recipes on a regular basis to make sure they're still good.

Mom, who gave me every single good food memory from my childhood—whether she made it at home, snagged it from a store, took us out for a treat, or tried to hide it from us in the freezer. (Behind the peas, mom? Amateur.) With those delicious childhood memories in mind, I wrote most of the recipes in this book.

Lindsay, Brian, Megan, and the entire Blue Star Press team. Thank you for finding me, loving this idea, throwing yourselves into it, and teaching me how to photograph food. I had no idea it would be this much fun to write a book with you! You're a talented, thoughtful bunch of people that I've only met on Zoom. Will it be weird when we meet in person?? I'm really tall, FYI (just so you're not freaked out later). Lindsay and Brian, special thanks to you for making me sound like a good writer.

My original L.A. roomies: Jess, Andrew (Poboy Boy), Lace, and Logan. Thank you for filling my cup with friendship and support and dog hair so that I could go on to create my dream restaurant, and ultimately, this dream cookbook. And thanks for eating all 60+ tester versions of my jambalaya recipe so I didn't have to feel bad about throwing it out.

My new friends (whom I've yet to meet), who picked up this book and decided to read the acknowledgments even though you're definitely not in them and you have no idea who I am. I feel like there's probably a lot of you people out there...now I'm curious. I'm going to start reading the acknowledgments first in books just to see what that's all about. Have you ever selected a book just from reading the acknowledgments? Thank you for prompting me to try something new...I'd never considered this way of living.

About the Author

Krimsey Lilleth is a writer, chef, and vegan food enthusiast living in North Hollywood, California. The founder of Krimsey's Cajun Kitchen ("The World's First Cajun Vegan Restaurant"), Lilleth built a loyal following of celebrities and everyday foodies in southern California who came to love her Cajun vegan cuisine. A native of Baton Rouge, Louisiana, and a former petroleum engineer, Lilleth has taken a series of twists, turns, and adventures that led her to where she is today. Her life and her work are driven by a desire to always be brave, take new risks, and try new things. She hopes her story will inspire others to step outside their comfort zones and boldly chase whatever life is calling them to do.

These days, Lilleth is still dreaming up new vegan recipes, now often focusing on whole foods. She also continues to follow her entrepreneurial calling, involving herself in new business start-ups related to waste reduction, green energy/nuclear power, vegan food/fitness, and general human welfare.

INDEX

INDEX

INDEX